W9-DFO-001

Who Cares for Planet Earth?

THE CON IN CONSERVATION

African elephant (*Loxodonta africana*)

Who Cares for Planet Earth?

THE CON IN CONSERVATION

Dr Bill Jordan

2 4 6 8 10 9 7 5 3 1
First published 2001 in Great Britain by
THE ALPHA PRESS
Box 2950
Brighton BN2 5SP

and in the United States of America by
THE ALPHA PRESS
5824 N.E. Hassalo St.
Portland, Oregon 97213-3644

British Library Cataloguing in Publication Data
A CIP catalogue record for this book is available from the British Library.

Library of Congress Cataloging-in-Publication Data
Jordan, Bill, 1941–
Who cares for planet Earth?: the CON in conservation/Bill Jordan.
p. cm.
Includes bibliographical references and index.
ISBN 1-898595-35-6 (alk. paper)
1. Human ecology. 2. Conservation of natural resources. 3. Environmental policy. I. Title.
GF41 .J665 2001
333.7'2—dc21 00-048535

Printed by Bookcraft, Midsomer Norton, Bath
This book is printed on acid-free paper

Contents

Foreword

Dr Richard Leakey

Rhetoric, wild promises, bold statements . . . there is a problem and we all know that there is a global overload of statements which promise action but the good intentions are as far as it goes. This is particularly true in the broad and critical area of the environment and conservation where countless international gatherings pledge the speakers to actions that seldom materialize.

Are these pledges made in good faith or is it, as suggested in the sub-title of this book, *The CON in Conservation*, simply a ritual or worse, a political strategy for short-term advantage? Does the press adequately audit performance? This is a legitimate concern and I have certainly listened to a good number of people who are very cynical indeed about the agenda being followed by the world's leaders in the political/conservation/environment debate.

This book sets forth some strong opinions which will not be shared by all who read them. Can zoos really help? Should the concept of progress be redefined and what are reasonable parameters for the world's population to sustain itself in terms of a consumptive, materialistic, universal culture? Can a hungry unemployed citizen share the concerns of the advocates for conservation of biodiversity? Indeed one might ask whether such a person can afford not to? Such issues do trouble many people and this book will certainly provoke debate. I recommend it and hope that through debate we might make a little more progress.

Preface

Society is being "conned" into believing that the destruction and pollution of natural life support systems is now recognised and is being rectified, and that development is sustainable. Nothing can be further from the truth. There are serious flaws in current thinking, much misinformation, lies and unfulfilled promises. Nasty facts are being omitted from the arguments to justify profit.

HISTORY OF CONSERVATION

Before the Second World War few people thought about conservation of natural resources, or even of man-made structures such as castles or bridges. Immediately after the war ended many people were eager to replace the old. They wanted to put all the horrors behind them and build a new world. The raw materials – such as oil, trees and animal skins – were available for mankind to use. Few thought they could be exhaustible.

Of course, areas of land had been protected in some countries for many years. This, however, was not a conservation measure in the broad sense, for many of these were simply "play" areas for hunting and later for tourism.

In 1911 the colonial government of Kenya enacted a treaty with the Maasai people after the Laikipia Maasai had been moved to the south of the new railway line to make way for European settlement. Finally, in 1948, the Amboseli National Reserve was declared. In the

Wildlife reserves in India often became the hunting grounds for Indian princes and the wealthy British colonials

same year the National Parks Act[1] became law in Britain. However, simply declaring an area to be a reserve or a national park does not mean the resources therein will be protected. In fact, in India reserves became the hunting grounds of the British and rich Indian princes who shot thousands of tigers and elephants. In America, in their war with the resident Indians, the immigrant settlers attempted to starve the Indians by slaughtering the buffalo – their main food animal, better known as the bison. It is estimated that by 1889 all but 2,000 or so of the 100 million had been killed, and little use was made of the carcasses. The passenger pigeon was one of the most common birds in America. Flocks of these birds were so large that they cast long shadows and took three hours to pass. Some of these huge flocks contained up to 1 billion birds. Within 20 years this species was extinct, largely through hunting. It is estimated that about one-quarter of all bird species have become extinct as a result of human actions.

In 1872, when Senator Haydon in the United States of America saw the scenic wonders of the Yellowstone region, he persuaded the US Congress to declare the area a national park. In the 1890s, more areas were set aside and could not be sold to logging companies. This was preservation of course, not conservation, because nearly everyone believed that nature's bounty should be used, and many still do! President Theodore Roosevelt, during his term of office (1901 to 1909), believed in, and promoted, the scientific management of nature's resources. His motive was to preserve wilderness and the animals it contained, for hunting.

CHANGES IN ATTITUDE

In the course of time economic gain became the main motive for conservation. According to Myers[2] we are now losing one species of mammal or bird life every year. The rate of loss due to human interference between the 1600s and 1900 was roughly one species every four years. In fact, since 1900 man has eliminated around 75 known species, almost all of them mammals and birds. But hardly anything is known about how many other creatures may have become extinct. While it is true to say that at least 90% of all species that have existed have disappeared, mainly through natural processes, it is only in the recent past, in the 10,000 years since man invented agriculture and ceased to be a hunter-gatherer, that he has caused the extinction of the greatest number of species, either by over hunting or by causing a loss of habitat.

The United States once had about 1 million square kilometres of natural prairie. Almost all of it has disappeared under agriculture.
In 1974 scientists gathered to discuss the problem and agreed that the extinction rate of all species could now have reached 1,000 per

year. Myers[3] considers this figure too low because the tropical moist forests are believed to contain between 2 million and 5 million species, and with areas of virgin forests in Brazil equal to the size of Switzerland being logged and burnt every year, it is probable that the rate of extinction is higher.

THE IMPACT OF SCIENCE AND TECHNOLOGY

All this has been brought about by advances in science. In one sense we cannot blame science, for it is simply a method of investigation and verification. But we can blame some of the scientists and certainly the purposes to which science has been put.

We are aware of course of the great benefits brought by science, for example the motor vehicle, without which cities are not possible. We are aware of the "green revolution" created by genetic selection of food plants to make them even more productive, which has doubled the amount of food the world produces. We are told of the great advances in pest control in food production, without which a third of the world's human population would starve. But we forget, or are not told full details of, the pollution that the motor vehicle creates, the greenhouse warming in the atmosphere and the destruction of the ozone layer, and the pollution caused by many pesticides which have now been banned in developed countries but are still used in the undeveloped.

The human population is increasing exponentially and the scientists are struggling to produce enough food and at the same time provide all the consumables that the wealthy nations demand. And while the research for ways of producing more food continues, productive soil is being lost through erosion or desertification. When the Greeks first used science it was coupled with philosophy. This is no longer the case; and in truth this is perhaps the real problem.

The genie has been let out of the bottle and we now have no control over it. We don't even know where science/technology will take us. The larger part of the population live in cities and interact with a man-made reality. They are told that science/technology means progress and progress is good and if problems do arise science will solve them.

Science works by dissection, by taking things apart. But when a beautiful valley or a flower is analysed into its respective parts – soil, rocks, rivers, trees, grass, colour and scent – we've lost the essence and the beauty that once was there. We have an objective analysis but the real meaning to us as living beings has gone. People believe that science is neutral and that the problem is how it is used or abused. On the other hand, science is a seductive temptress. Once a scientist begins a research programme it receives his or her full attention so that the individual no longer feels able to say "No" to the study of matters which might otherwise not appeal. The study as a whole then becomes a rationialisation for finding merit in the study. For example, it is said that half the scientists in the western world are employed on what are called "defence projects". However, it is well known that during the past two decades many wars have been fought by poor countries with weapons supplied by rich countries.

The development of powerful methods of extraction of natural resources has encouraged a belief that with science and technology the entire planet can be managed and controlled. Unfortunately this is a delusion with far-reaching consequences.

SUSTAINABLE USE

In the course of time, economic gain has become the main goal. The aims of conservation have narrowed to those that have a direct benefit for humans in the form of jobs, wealth creation and development. "No free lunch" has become the motto. All conservation has to include a human benefit. Eventually the concept was kidnapped by those who exploit natural resources, to provide a caption coined by a group called "The Wise Use Movement". Even the International Union for the Conservation of Nature and Natural Resources (IUCN) produced a book on sustainable development called World Conservation Strategy. It's like saying to a thief, "You can take some, but not all". To many people, this philosophy seems logical and even reasonable. The British government, when Margaret Thatcher was Prime Minister, told the UK Natural Environment Research Council that the research it funded must lead to wealth creation.[4] The policy has continued and, according to a recent statement, one of their aims is to contribute to Britain's economic competitiveness. This is economic sustainability – not ecological sustainability.

There is a similar policy in Europe. The European Union has stated, in its research agenda for 1999 to 2002, that the priority is "to link the ability to discover to the ability to produce . . . leading to wealth creation".[5] Apart from the fact that this approach is very much one sided, its effects on the environment are not costed properly. To the cost of all industrial processes must be added the cost of preventing pollution. Agriculture must be sustainable and so must fisheries. At the same time, neither the land nor the sea should be polluted just because that happens to be the cheapest and easiest method of getting rid of waste.

Once a price has been put on it the environment becomes a commodity to be exploited and the emphasis is placed on sustainable harvesting. Who is to say what is sustainable and how such a decision can be enforced? The result is that conservation is applied only to those animals and plants that have a value for humans. Aldo Leopold,[6] an American forester, argued that all species should have a

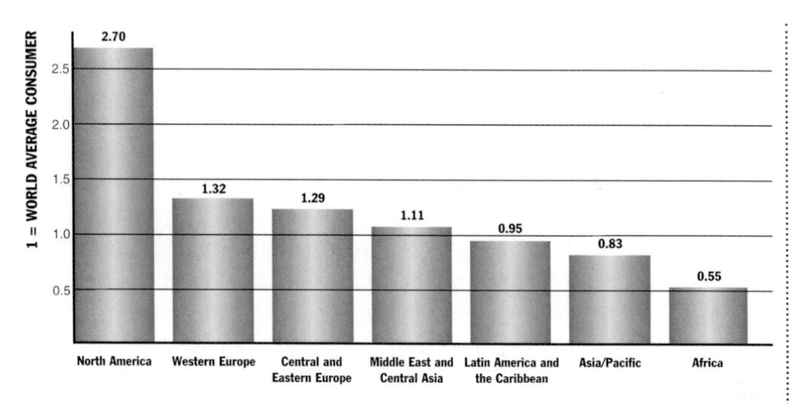

Figure 0.1: Consumption of natural resources: unit per person per year, 1995

value independent of their value to humans. He wrote: "a system of conservation based solely on economic self interest is hopelessly lopsided. It tends to ignore, and thus eventually eliminate many elements in the land that lack commercial value, but that are essential to its healthy functioning."

One value that is never costed is the spiritual. Many people go to the countryside for rest and recreation; many people bring plants and flowers into their houses for the pleasure they promote.

THE EFFECTS OF POPULATION GROWTH

Though the growth of the world's human population has been slowing in industrial countries, there are many other countries where the population will double in 20 or 30 years. Consumerism is accelerating and putting an increasing strain on natural resources and waste disposal. As developing countries become more industrial their demands on resources and the resulting pollution will grow.

Exponential growth means that if the demand for resources doubles in a year, the annual need is equal to that of all the previous years put together. We are acting today as if all natural resources are infinite. Indeed the accepted economic philosophy is that growth will produce wealth, more jobs and what is called a higher standard of living – which really means possessing more consumables. The important question is: Can the planet sustain the western quality of life for all people, with the pollution and ecological damage that would ensue? The answer is plainly "No!" Doesn't economic growth mean more use of natural resources and more waste and pollution?

Many business people regard natural resources as free and think their only costs are labour energy and the capital cost of extraction. They usually feel no obligation to seek ways of conservation or replacement, and if they are required to limit pollution, they complain it will reduce profits and put up prices. At the same time, governments are promoting sustainable use. But what is meant by "sustainable" when many of the resources humans use are non-renewable?

"Not so!" say many scientists. The price of oil fell in recent years because of a glut. However, since then it has risen because major oil producing countries reduced extraction. Though more oil is being discovered every year it is not a renewable source of energy. It doesn't matter, say the scientists, because we are finding alternatives to non-renewable resources and their use can be scientifically controlled by the formula called "maximum sustainable yield". The theory is based on the assumption that there is always a surplus of renewable resources be they from plants or animals. If the amount of this surplus is known it can be harvested, which will reduce competition for food, and this will stimulate production. For example, if a population of a species is reduced to 75% of its original size, more food will be available for those remaining and reproduction will be stimulated to make up the numbers, which in turn can be harvested annually. The theory sounds logical, but does it work? The answer is "No", because there are unpredictable events, like drought, disease and reproductive failure. In any case enforcement of such a policy is almost impossible because of over-exploitation.

ATTEMPTS AT LEGISLATION

The International Whaling Commission was formed in 1948 to control whaling so that harvesting could continue forever. Unfortunately its history has been one of "too little too late". The International Whaling Commission's scientific committee estimated the numbers of animals in each population and set limits on what can be taken. But pirate whaling continued. Whalers ignored the controls in some instances and refused to have foreign national inspectors on board their ships. Several species of cetaceans are threatened with extinction and still their annual slaughter continues. After the fall of the communist regime in Russia we learnt that Russian whalers were secretly killing the blue whale although it was officially protected by all members of the International Whaling Commission, including Russia.

Commercial fishing is another example of the failure of legislation. Several common species have been harvested almost to extinction. First the anchovies, upon which millions of birds fed, were harvested in greater and greater quantities until the fishery collapsed. Then it was the turn of the herring, and now the cod fisheries are collapsing in spite of controls and recommended good practice. The scientists can say that their advice has not been followed. However, events like the sudden change in climate caused by the El Niño effect can upset the most careful calculations. It is no comfort to know that two-thirds of the major marine fisheries are either fully exploited or over exploited. Many are seriously depleted following the onslaught of modern industrial techniques, which are facilitating the catching of fish faster than the fish can reproduce. These techniques include long lines measuring up to 120 kilometres, with thousands of hooks on them, and drift nets up to 60 kilometres long that hang down from the surface of the sea. These catch indiscriminately so that non-target species such as turtles, seals, dolphins, whales and birds (to mention only a few species) are killed (the "bykill") and discarded. Modern electronic navigation aids and satellite positioning systems can take ships to where shoals of fish have been spotted from aircraft.

In some fisheries the bykill exceeds the catch. In the Gulf of Mexico 2,000,000 snappers and 2,800 metric tons of sharks are caught annually and thrown away. Trawling for shrimps kills between two and eight times more creatures than the actual catch of shrimps. The shrimp cocktail on your table is the cause of much destruction of marine life.

But the best known bykill is the 40,000 dolphin killed annually by fishermen hunting the yellowfin tuna. They would find the tuna by seeking the dolphins feeding on them. They would then encircle both tuna and dolphin with a huge net and haul the whole lot on board. In 30 years the eastern spinner dolphin population was reduced by 80%.

To add insult to injury, fish prices are kept down by subsidies, which distorts the economics that would otherwise make such intensive fishing less profitable, and might bring about a decline. But again, jobs are at stake, and boats and equipment have to be paid for and profits have to be made. The driving force is money; as Ghandi said, "Greed, not need." In response, those involved will argue that jobs, i.e. people's livelihood, have to be protected. So when a target species crashes, a new target species is found, as happened with cod. When the species became rare due to over fishing the industry concentrated on other species.

The "jobs versus environment" argument is really the choice between short-term gain and long-term sustained use. The argument which many use, that prosperity may be hindered by conservation of natural resources, is false in the long term. Clear-cutting forests or burning them to plant crops can have costly consequences. A good example is the effect on the water supply for New York City. According to Chichilnisky and Heal,[7] the watershed which provided a natural filtration system free of charge for the water for New York became overwhelmed by sewage and farm run-off when the forest was felled. To buy and restore the watershed was going to cost US $1 billion, but to build a filtration and purification plant would cost US $6 to $8 billion.

We ignore, and fail to conserve the planet's life-support systems. "People first" sounds reasonable and logical, and surely some account should be taken of human nature, but this seems not to be the case if one considers international trade agreements, such as NAFTA (North American Free Trade Agreement), and GATT (General Agreement on Tariffs and Trade). Trade is now supreme, and protected from all threats that might interfere with it. So, for example, carpets made with child labour or slave labour can freely enter world trade. Animal products coming from systems that are cruel cannot be blocked by a country with good animal welfare standards. So the effect is to lower, not raise, standards. If a country exports natural products that are endangered, then importing countries cannot refuse to accept them. GATT is enforced by the World Trade Organisation, which is an unelected bureaucracy that deliberates in private. A recent example of its operation was the European Union directive passed by a large majority in the European Parliament in 1991 to ban the importation of fur from animals caught in cruel traps. Under the threat of being taken to court by Canada and the USA, the European Union caved in. Importation continues.

The use of pesticides that have a knock-on effect on other species has been shown to have damaging effects on conservation. The extensive use of DDT caused fragile eggs and lower reproduction in many wild bird species. Pollution by chemicals can have serious effects on wildlife. PCBs (poly chlorinated biphenols) are known to damage both the immune and the reproductive systems of marine mammals. Very little discussion, and almost no effort is put into controls in the name of conservation.

A thousand or so new chemicals are being produced each year, and only a few are monitored. The biological effects, especially possible synergistic effects, are unknown. We know that PCBs affect the reproductive system. But how many people know that some modern synthetic chemicals, for example polystyrene and PVC, mimic the female hormone oestrogen? Many of these chemicals are more than a thousand times more powerful than oestradiol and are responsible for sexual abnormalities in fish. Recently, falling sperm counts in men have been discovered. The average decline has been 50% between 1940 and 1990 in the western world.

Another "con" in conservation is the lack of consideration for the ecological systems that act as life-support services. Water is purified by natural processes, waste is decomposed, fertility of the soil is maintained, plants are pollinated, not to mention the protection by the ozone layer from harmful ultraviolet rays. Yet in the interest of profits and jobs these natural processes are being damaged. Water is being contaminated by industrial processes, waste is not being disposed of properly, monoculture with the same crop year after year, together with the use of chemicals to kill pests, is destroying the soil. The most that happens is a series of conferences, scientific papers, talks and reports. When the participants return home it is business as usual. Conservation receives only lip service, while the public focuses attention on saving a few popular species, usually mammals and birds.

Can we learn the truth about environmental problems from the media when we know they are owned by large corporations? In the USA the National Broadcasting Company is owned by General Electric, and Group W Television is owned by Westinghouse. Large multinational companies are often active in the Third World, some in the arms trade. Is it likely that a newspaper or TV station owned by a multinational company would allow significant coverage of what could be against their interests? Is it not possible that ownership could influence the media content because, after all, it relies heavily on advertising?

Mark Curtis, in his book *Ambiguities of Power*,[8] says that *The Times*, the *Telegraph* and the *Financial Times* "systematically fail to elucidate the specific link between British policy and human rights abuses". He goes on to say, "these newspapers are firmly entrenched within a propaganda system and their reporting implicitly serves to promote the concept of Britain's basic benevolence". I believe this also applies to major environmental abuses. At an international meeting to discuss tiger conservation, organized and paid for by Exxon, the representatives of the company were asked in a plenary meeting: "would it refrain from exploiting an oil reserve if it was in a tiger sanctuary?" No one spoke. The question was never answered. What hope is there for real conservation?

Does anyone really care about conservation of our environment? Many people express their concern. World Environment Day is celebrated on the 5th of June every year. Conferences are held, eloquent speeches made, and there is media interest. Then all is forgotten till the following year. Yet everyone knows the forests are disappearing. Everyone can smell the pollution in the air. We all shrug our shoulders and mutter "What can I do?"

The planet is known as Mother Earth, so perhaps the time has come for women to take control of conservation.

Notes

1. E. Huxley, *Nine Faces of Kenya*. HarperCollins, 1990.
2. N. Myers, *The Sinking Ark*. Pergamon Press, 1979.
3. Ibid.
4. J. Gray Forum, "Protect and survive". *New Scientist*, vol. 159, no. 2147, p. 48.
5. Ibid.
6. Aldo Leopold, *A Sand County Almanac*. Ballantine, 1949.
7. Chichilnisky and Heal, cited by J. Lubchenco, in *Resurgence*, no. 190, pp. 12–18.
8. Mark Curtis, cited in X. Edwards, "Can we learn the truth about the environment from the media". *The Ecologist*, vol. 28, pp. 18–22.

Acknowledgements

The editor and publisher gratefully acknowledge the following for permission to reproduce copyright material:

Chapter 7: The Introduction to Creda Mutwa's book *Isilwane – The Animal* is reprinted here by kind permission of Struik Publishers.

Chapter 8: Credo Mutwa and Struik Publishers for the kind permission to quote from Credo's book *Isilwane*; the extract from David Western, *In the Dust of Kilimanjaro*, © David Western, is reproduced with kind permission of the publisher, Island Press, Washington, D.C. and Covelo, CA; Gareth Patterson would also like to thank the University of Natal Press for permission to reprint material from *The Kruger National Park – a Social and Political History*, by Jane Carruthers.

Bill Jordan would like to thank Dr M. H. Woodford for his invaluable advice, Julia Robinson for proof-reading, Sandra Ferry for typing numerous drafts, Steve Hilling for original designs, and Care For The Wild International for permission to use photographic material.

The editor and publisher apologizes for any errors or omissions in the above acknowledgements and would be grateful to be notified of any corrections that should be incorporated in the next edition or reprint of this book.

The wildlife of today is not ours to dispose of as we please. We have it in trust. We must account for it to those who come after.

King George VI

'Twere all as good to ease one beast of grief.
As sit and watch the sorrows of the world.

Edwin Arnold

Our deepest fear is not that we are inadequate, it is that we are powerful beyond measure.

Nelson Mandela

The greatness of a nation and its moral progress can be judged by the way its animals are treated.

Mahatma Gandhi

We need another and a wiser, and perhaps a more mystical concept of animals. For the animal shall not be measured by man. They are not brethren. They are not underlings. They are other nations caught with ourselves in the net of life and time.

Henry Beston

Animals too have souls.

Pope John Paul II

The unpardonable forgetfulness in which the lower animals have hitherto been left by the moralists of Europe is well known. It is pretended that the beasts have no rights. They persuade themselves that our conduct in regard to them has nothing to do with morals or (to speak the language of their morality) that we have no duties towards animals; a doctrine revolting, gross and barbarous.

Arthur Schopenhauer

To see and not observe through memory is knowing. To hear and note the silence of the world is praying. To love and not know why or ask is living. To be and not desire or have is growing.

Bill Jordan

What we know, what we think, what we believe, is in the end of little consequence. *The only thing of consequence is what we do.*

Who Cares for Planet Earth?

THE CON IN CONSERVATION

1 Human Impact

Bill Jordan

Who cares for Planet Earth? There are some people who do but are frustrated by unfulfilled promises. There are many who have doubts about the assurances that problems are being solved and many more who are confused and feel too helpless to bother. There are some who have either convinced themselves that solutions are being found to deal with exploitation and pollution or they simply don't care. The impact of humans on the planet is very great and increasing. Society is being "conned" into believing that all is well with planet Earth, that all development is sustainable, that science can rectify past mistakes and that politicians are taking the necessary steps. Nothing can be further from the truth. The planet lies haemorrhaging and poisoned by man-made pollution. Serious flaws in current thinking, a lack of clear logic coupled with much misinformation, unfulfilled promises and lies are exposed.

Twenty million tons of people was Myer's[1] estimate of the weight of all the people in the world 20 years ago, all balanced on the pinnacle of life and sustained by myriads of organisms and plants recycling nutrients and purifying water. The world is even more crowded today.

POPULATION

Every second between 4 or 5 babies are born, 260,000 each day, an increase of 100 million each year.

For sure the world is a big place, but for how long can it sustain the addition of four times the population of Canada or almost twice that of Britain each year?

In spite of a drop in fertility rates, the growth in population continues in developing countries. The fact that human population size has reached a peak and is now stable in many, but not all, developed western countries gives some hope that this can happen in the rest of the world. But the urge to have children is great and many people are opposed to abortion and contraception. Indeed in May 1990 in Mexico, Pope John Paul II preached a sermon against birth control, saying that if the possibility of conceiving is artificially blocked the people involved are cutting themselves off from God and are opposing His will. In the West, expensive medical techniques are being used to help childless couples conceive, and the Canadian government has expressed its concern about the falling birth rate in a booklet called "From Baby Boom To Baby Bust".

In most of the world, infertility is not a problem and more humans are added to the world population at an ever increasing rate. It's hard to fully appreciate the huge numbers involved such as Kenya doubling its population every 17 years, and every year an extra 100 million people in the world. In India alone the human population is increasing at the rate of over 70,000, or another medium-size town, every day.

E. O. Wilson, in his recent book *In Search of Nature*,[2] gives a good illustration of growth in numbers by way of the French riddle of the lily pond. At first there was only one lily pad. Next day and every subsequent day it, and its descendants, doubled, until on the 30th day the pond was full. When was it half full? The answer is "on day 29". This is what Suzuki[3] describes as "exponential growth". So a 4% growth in human population would mean a doubling every 17½ years, which means in those 17½ years as many people would be added as there were at the beginning.

According to an article in a 1990 issue of *People*[4] there were 600 million people living in towns and cities in 1950; now there are probably 2½ billion – nearly half the world's total population. Nevertheless, increasing urbanization doesn't relieve pressure on land, because people need food and clothing and many can afford, and want, consumables. More people, more consumables, more trade, more profit.

In 1990 it was estimated that 75% of Latin America's population would be urbanized by the year 2000. In Africa the figure would be 42% and in Asia 37%. The reason for the migration to the cities is the search for work. Many, however, have found only grinding poverty. We are told their only hope of improvement is development, this means industrialization and increased consumerism. According to the United Nations Population Fund one-third of the total population of the world is under 15 years old. The fundamental questions are: Can they all be fed, and how will the environment be affected?

THE LAND

More land is needed for crops, yet 6 million hectares of good agricultural land are being lost annually. One-third of the world's land surface is threatened with desertification and over 20 million hectares of tropical rainforest are being destroyed every year together with the species they contain.

The year 1985 was a bumper year for crop production. It could have provided a vegetarian diet for 6 billion people. Because a large proportion of the harvest was used for animal feed to produce the animal products that make up 35% of the western diet, the bumper crop could only feed 2½ billion.

Even if food could be fairly distributed production must be increased – but can it be?

In 1798 an English clergyman called Malthus observed that peasants were having trouble feeding their children because family size had been increasing for the previous 50 years. He concluded that the population increase was exceeding the power of the Earth to produce subsistence for man. He predicted a famine, but it never occurred because the land was made more productive by improvements in farming.

PRODUCTION AND DEMAND

In 1972, the Club of Rome predicted a famine because the increasing numbers of people on Earth were greater than the necessary amount of food which could be produced. Once again, changing to higher yielding crop varieties, chemical fertilizers, pest control and irrigation(collectively called the "green revolution"), averted disaster. Grain production increased by 3% each year from 1950 to 1983. By the mid-1980s there were huge grain surpluses, meat and butter mountains and milk lakes. The big question today is: Has food production reached a peak? On paper it seems that if the world population peaked at 10 billion in 2050 and there was an increase of 12 million tonnes of grain each year, and we all stopped eating animal products, there would be just enough food for everyone, i.e. 244 kilogrammes per person per annum.

But the low prices of grain do not encourage maximum yields and farmers in Britain and Europe are subsidized to let the land lie fallow. Growing prosperity in China and India means that many of their citizens are buying animal products. In addition their farmland is gradually diminishing for several reasons, such as the growth of urban centres. So the USA, and, to a lesser extent, Europe, makes up the deficiency in grain production in China, India and Africa. At the same time Third World countries are forced to grow cash crops for export to pay off debts. A poor harvest in any of these countries could have a disastrous effect because there are no grain mountains.

In a recent article Dr Myers[5] points out that if every Chinese person was to eat just one more chicken per year, the grain consumed would equal the total grain export of Canada. Americans eat an average of 45 kilos of beef each year. If the Chinese were to eat a similar amount instead of the 4 kilos per year they now eat, it would take the entire grain harvest of the United States of America.

The problem, largely ignored, is that there are growing numbers of Chinese, Indians, Asians and non-Europeans who demand, and can afford to pay for, this increased consumption.

The green revolution seems to have peaked. The increase in production year on year has dropped to 1%. Biotechnology might produce better productive strains of grain but no one believes it will have a significant effect. Redesigning the rice plant by crossing two major species could give possibly a 20% greater yield. But it can only be grown in irrigated lowland fields, which provide only one-third of the world crop. Coupled with this is a continual fight against pests and diseases.

FERTILIZERS AND PESTICIDES: CHEMICAL THREATS TO CONSERVATION

Artificial fertilizers are necessary in greater and greater amounts to produce crops on this scale. The main component of fertilizers is nitrogen, which is essential to plants for making proteins. Indeed until ammonia was synthesized, food production was limited because the only source of nitrogen for most plants was animal and human waste. Using crop rotation, and legumes, which have nitrogen-fixing bacteria in their roots, one acre of soil could only feed three people. In the 19th century the critical role of nitrogen, phosphorus and potassium in food production was discovered. Potash, phosphate and nitrogen salts were mined and spread on the fields. In addition, the enormous deposits of seabird excreta (guano) from Peru provided a natural source of nitrogen.

Then in 1899, Bosch discovered how to synthesize ammonia; by 1913 Haber had devised a method to produce it on an industrial scale. By the late 1940s, 5 million tons were being used as fertilizer. Today around 175 million tons of nitrogen fertilizer are used, which provides about 40% of all nitrogen taken up by crops. Artificial fertilizers permit the production of sufficient extra food for about 2 billion people.

There is, however, a down side. Not only is ammonia synthesis based on non-renewable energy, but unfortunately the use of these massive amounts of nitrogen salts has serious consequences for the environment. Nitrates can leach into the ground water and cause "blue baby" disease and possibly some cancers. In some ponds and lakes the growth of algae and proliferation of cyanobacteria starves fish and crustacea of oxygen. Plagues of these organisms are found in the San Francisco Bay, the Baltic Sea and Australia's Great Barrier Reef.

More insidiously, the nitrogen compounds make the soil acid, which in turn allows the release of dangerous heavy metals and causes the loss of essential trace elements. Finally, nitrous oxide is released into the air and contributes to the destruction of ozone, which protects life from dangerous ultraviolet rays, and also contributing to greenhouse warming.

There is no means of growing crops on the present-day scale without nitrogen fertilizer, so conservation is sacrificed.

There is one further irony. High yields have meant low iron content in the crops in South Asia in particular. In that region there is now a pandemic of anaemia affecting 1.5 billion children, and causing poor mental and motor skills.

One suggestion is to farm more land, but many people fear that this would be at the expense of wildlife. However, there is little worthwhile land left for farming. Only about 11% of land in the world is suitable for farming in any case. Wildlife is left in peace for the present because the territory it occupies is not fit for farming. In fact land suitable for growing grain is shrinking, and by 2050 there will probably be only one-quarter acre per person.

Intensive farming depletes the soil and the water supply. Seven million hectares of soil are lost to agriculture each year through erosion. This represents 0.5% of all farmland – a considerable loss. Most of this soil ends up in the sea.

In affluent countries farmland is being built upon at a rate of about a million acres per year, which means two acres of good agricultural land are lost every minute to urban sprawl.

Changes in the microbiology of soil in Pakistan, India, Nepal and Bangladesh, due to the use of pesticides and monoculture, have halted annual increases in yields.

The lesson of DDT (dichlorodiphenyltrichloroethane) is well known because of Rachel Carson's book *Silent Spring*,[6] but it is thought that this pesticide is still being manufactured and used in some Third World countries. Although it was banned in the early 1970s in North America after it had spread worldwide from where it was being used, there are significant amounts in the Arctic, for example in polar bears, seals and fish. Eskimos have been warned not to eat too much seal meat and fish. Breakdown products from DDT have now been detected in the fluid surrounding the foetus in pregnant women. One of these breakdown products is DDE which can bind to and inactivate cell reception for the hormone testosterone, which plays an important part in the masculination of boys.

In a study into the decline of fish eagles at Lake Kariba in Zambia it was found that the shells of their eggs were 20% thinner than normal as a result of DDT and its derivatives, which had been used to control insects called glossina which transmit sleeping sickness. It was predicted that the bird could become locally extinct within 10 years if the use of DDT was not curtailed. Since 1946, Zimbabwe has been using 1,000 tons annually, half of which would have drained into Lake Kariba. Zimbabwe banned its use in gardens in 1973 but did not ban its use by the government to control tsetse fly, though the annual amount used has fallen to 300 tons annually.

Chlordane, and other man-made pesticides, have accumulated to dangerous levels in Arctic marine mammals even though they were banned for most purposes in 1987 though permitted for termite control.

In 1999 a cancer- causing poison called dioxin got into the food chain in Belgium and contaminated chicken's eggs and dairy products. To date, it has not been discovered how it got there. There remains the possibility that it may be a constant toxic ingredient in animal feed. In any case, dioxins are pumped into the atmosphere by incinerators. The French agriculture ministry have estimated that between 1,800 and 5,200 French people die from cancer caused by dioxins. In a less publicized event in 1992 in the United States, a national survey found high levels of the most toxic form of dioxin in a bentonite clay used as an anti-caking agent in soya meal fed to about 1fl million chickens over a period of several years.

WATER SUPPLIES

The other essential for intensive farming is water. Every year approximately 113,000 cubic kilometres of water falls as rain or snow on the continents – enough to cover the land surface of the Earth to a depth of 80 centimetres (over 2 feet). It is not spread evenly. Much of Africa, the Middle East, North Asia, western USA, parts of Argentina and Chile, and most of Australia get very little. Yet nearly 2 billion people live in these water-shortage areas. As the human population grows there is less water for each individual, less for crop growing, and less for wildlife. Much ground water has been contaminated and what is not poisoned is being depleted much faster than it can ever be replenished. The large aquifer below Birmingham in the United Kingdom is largely unusable because of contamination with chlorinated solvents. In recent years several large bore holes elsewhere have been shut because of solvent contamination. The situation is worse in other countries. Delhi has the reputation of being one of the world's dirtiest cities. The drinking water contains dangerously high levels of pesticides and heavy metals. Much of Delhi's sewage flows directly into the Yamuna River. The River Athi, which flows through Nairobi, is heavily contaminated and yet it is

Figure 1.1: Diagram showing average annual rainfall

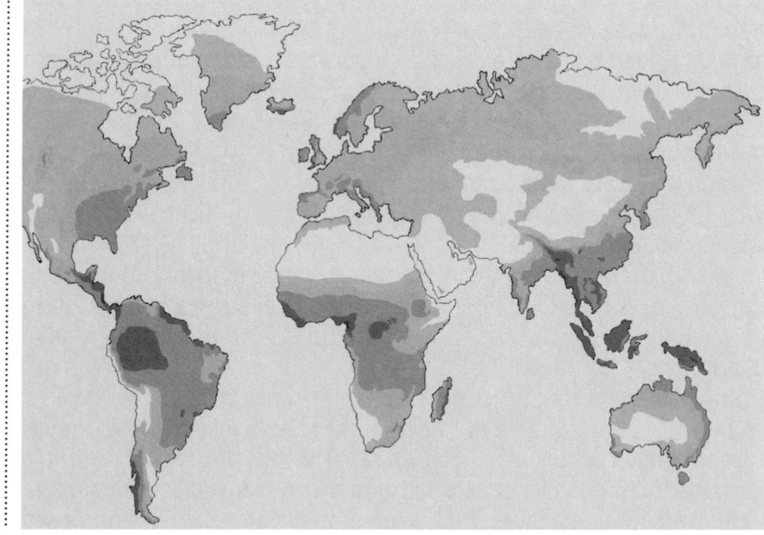

the main source of drinking water for people and wildlife as it flows south towards Tsavo.

Much of the contamination of water and soil comes from industry. Those people who have enough to eat are widening their expectations to include manufactured goods. Consumerism is being promoted as the cure for human problems. Consumerism means trade, leading to more production, more employment, and is labelled "progress". Happiness, it seems, depends on growth.

CONSUMERISM

In the past, supply usually followed demand. Now supply comes first, then advertising is used to create a demand. In this way new jobs are created in devising new consumables and new jobs in advertising to create the corresponding desires. More consumption equals more jobs, meaning prosperity. In its wake there is more pollution and more waste. Vaclav Havel,[7] the president of the Czech Republic, in an article in *Civilisation*, writes of the lack of responsibility for the planet. He says that rising production is considered to be the main sign of national success, not only in poor states but also in the wealthy ones, which "are cutting the branch on which they sit with their ideology of indefinitely prolonged and senseless growth". The attempts that are made to avert these dangers do not touch "the seed from which they sprout" but merely try to diminish their impact. He believes that in spite of the domination of a few major religious systems, civilization is now deeply atheistic for the first time in history.

Is it a "Catch 22" situation? As far as improving human welfare is concerned, there seems to be only one political goal, which is economic growth. Western societies are called consumer societies. The solution to poverty and starvation in developing countries is to encourage development, in other words to "be like us". Consumerism has been successful. It has brought benefits. Life is more comfortable for more people: there is better housing, better health, better diet and less drudgery, but not for everyone. The cost is social disruption and the annihilation of culture of some societies and the extinction of millions of species. Many people are unaware of these costs, principally the pressure on the natural environment. The message of the Rio Earth Summit in 1992 was that the future of the Earth is bleak and there is little time for change. The way things look at present is that change is unlikely. China, containing one-sixth of all humans on Planet Earth, has learnt from the West that the planet is consumable and the Chinese will therefore soon be the leading producers of greenhouse gases as they proceed to manufacture and provide washing machines, fridges, TVs, cars, and all the other goodies valued in the West.

Global consumption of goods and services reached a staggering total of US $24 trillion, six times the total for 1975. Such unchecked consumption threatens the environment in many ways. For example, if the Chinese were to have the same per capita car ownership as the United States, their oil consumption would be greater than total world consumption today – the potential for pollution is staggering.

THE COSTS

Progress is a cultural, comfortable affliction for now. Is there a cure? Is a cure necessary? And if so, what is it? Many people know the dangers: 50 million acres of forest cut each year, millions of acres of farmland destroyed or washed away, most of the major fisheries in serious decline, and pollution of the air, sea and land – and yet we still believe in progress. Is it conformity, resignation or stupidity? Or is it a mixture of all three? Stupidity seems to be distributed in a constant proportion in all groups and strata of all societies. Stupid people create problems without any benefit to themselves. What they say or promote can seem reasonable simply because they appear to have nothing to gain and seem to be acting in a selfless manner. We are thus deceived. It doesn't occur to us that they may be stupid, especially if they are well read and knowledgeable. So we, like sheep, follow not realizing how dangerous stupid people really are. They sound convincing because they are so positive. Take, for example, the politicians who allow fish stocks or any species to be destroyed to save jobs. They have little to gain except popularity, and jobs which are preserved temporarily. But the ultimate loss is forever.

Items that reduce drudgery and improve comforts are now considered an essential part of life. But what about "toys"? Do we really need all the items that amuse or distract us for the moment? The eminent psychologist Abraham Maslow[8] describes what he calls the hierarchy of needs. The basic needs are hunger, thirst and safety. Then there is a need for love and belonging. And when these are satisfied the need for self-respect and self-esteem, and the esteem of others comes to the fore. It is at this level that consumerism enters, in the form of "I've got more stuff and better stuff than my acquaintances". It also encompasses curiosity and the acquisition of knowledge. Many people never pass this stage. Maslow describes a higher need – that of what he calls self-actualization. A flavour of what he means may be gained from the statement of Einstein: "The most beautiful thing we can experience is the mysterious. It is the source of all art and science." In short, it means the ability to fulfil your potential, whatever that may be.

So convinced are governments (encouraged by manufacturing companies) that consumerism means progress and the good life for all, that they have signed the General Agreement on Tariffs and Trade (GATT) and set up the World Trade Organisation. The WTO is an organization which limits national sovereignty. Many measures that now protect the environment could be banned. Even trade in goods produced by slave labour or child labour cannot be prohibited. So the bulldozers and the chainsaws that are destroying rainforests, the huge trawlers ravaging the world's fish stocks, may be surpassed in global stupidity by middle-aged men in suits working in the WTO centre in Geneva. Unelected and immensely powerful, they are creating a world in which no one can interfere with trade. They can force countries which have banned particular products, because they are dangerous to the environment, to allow their importation, thus negating attempts for better standards. Their "trade rules" reduce all efforts for higher standards for human and animal welfare and environmental protection to the lowest common denominator – a single global economy. The WTO says it is no longer possible to distinguish products that are produced sustainably from those that are not. It does not allow a government to protect its citizens from a higher level of risk by banning the importation of products produced with lower standards. The first major example occurred in 1996, when a challenge was made by Venezuela and Brazil to the United States in connection with the Clean Air Act which banned importation of gasoline (petrol) which didn't meet its standards set to reduce air pollution. The WTO ruled in favour of the polluters. It therefore protects profits above the need to protect and conserve the environment of Planet Earth.

Pollution, whether by improper disposal of waste due to indifference, or through the misuse of poisonous chemicals by design, is beginning to have a more serious effect on the environment because the quantities are escalating and some are not biodegradable. Poly chlorinated biphenols (PCBs) used as a non conducting lubricant in electrical switching equipment is not biodegradable and remains toxic. Though production of this chemical has stopped there is still a significant quantity in use. As the equipment is replaced PCB's will be released into the environment unless great care is taken. They have a hormone-like action which interferes with reproduction and the immune response to disease. Already, marine mammals are showing signs of poor fertility and lower resistance. The great virus epidemic which killed thousands of seals and many dolphins a few years ago in the North Sea is believed to have been made possible by lowered resistance to disease. PCBs in the ageing tower blocks in Sweden are endangering human health and are now causing great concern. The Swedish authorities have said that the concentration of PCBs in the soil around the buildings is 20 times the safety limit.[9] In 1995 women who had eaten fish from the contaminated waters of the Great Lakes in Canada gave birth to babies with unusually high susceptibility to bacterial infection.

We now know a major cause of the serious decline in frogs in North America and perhaps in Britain too is a mosquito repellent and a flea powder containing S-Methoprene which breaks down in sunlight into retinoid compounds which are deadly to amphibia: 5 kilos of flea powder can poison 100,000 litres of water.

The developed countries contain about 20% of the world's human population and use over 70% of the world's resources. What will happen to these resources and the pollution resulting when the remaining 80% of humans reach western standards of consumption and pollution? At present the USA generates five tons of carbon per person while 2 billion Indians and Chinese generate half a ton per person. When these countries are fully industrialized, using the world's largest reserves of coal beneath their soil, the output of greenhouse gases will soar, and 40 years from now will be twice what it is today. Already we are experiencing global warming. So is there really a solution? Can meltdown of the polar ice and the climate disruption it will bring be avoided? Where does that leave all the noble talk of conservation at the many international conferences like Rio?

Worse still are the attempts to get rid of dangerous waste by dumping it in Third World countries. There have been toxic shipments from the industrial west to West Africa. Some have been completed, such as the estimated 10,000 large drums of toxic waste containing PCBs and heavy metals and solvents dumped in the village of Koko in Nigeria. They had been brought in using forged papers. Eventually the Nigerian government found out and persuaded the Italian government to take them back. Other proposed shipments were stopped, such as the deal for Congo to take a million tons of solvent from an obscure company registered in Liechtenstein. Gabon had agreed to take uranium tailings from the USA but later declined.

Now, not in my back yard (NIMBY) no longer has meaning because the world is everyone's back yard. In many countries there are local problems such as the explosion at Bophal, India in a foreign factory sited there because of cheap labour. An interesting and dangerous problem arose in North Carolina, USA, and was described in a book by Rodney Barker called *And The Waters Turned to Blood*. Giant cesspools attached to factory farms containing raw sewage equivalent to what might come from two cities the size of New York, burst and the contents poured into the rivers and estuaries. If that wasn't bad enough, a small creature called *Pfeisteria piscidida* found the pollution to its liking and multiplied enormously. It attacked and ate holes in fish and damaged the skin of unsuspecting humans.

Fish farms also pollute and are affecting the numbers of wild salmon in the seas off Scotland and Canada. Pesticides are affecting the fish in the remote Arctic and one chemical, Toxaphene, has been found in the breast milk of Innuit mothers, even though it has only been used extensively in Asia and Latin America. How many such problems exist unnoticed?

FORESTS

The planet is losing its tree cover. Not only are a hundred acres of tropical forest being destroyed every minute of every day, equal to an area larger than England and Wales each year and with them about 200,000 species annually, but trees are being felled in temperate countries to provide timber for building, wood for packing cases, for Japanese chopsticks and for paper. How many trees will be required for toilet paper when the two billion people in India and China change from using water to toilet paper?

A little known fact was recorded in a recent report by Helmut Geist.[10] He estimates that tobacco farmers clear 200,000 hectares of forest and woodland every year and account for 5% of deforestation in the worst affected countries, namely South Africa, Zimbabwe, Malawi, China, South Korea and Uruguay. Virgin forest provides the best land and wood to cure and store the crop.

Trees are being cut down in vast numbers in Third World countries simply to burn for cooking food. Three billion people depend on wood for all their household energy. Forests are being destroyed without a second thought. Nature reserves are being eaten away by the surrounding people. They have no other form of energy. The loss of trees for all these reasons seems unstoppable and the effect on wildlife is disastrous.

The quality of most of the planet's forests is declining as loggers concentrate on the best forests and cut the best trees such as in Canada, Siberia, the Arctic regions and the tropics. Air pollution in Europe is damaging trees, causing a decline in the quality of forests and the death of many trees. Because of the demand for wood, the logging companies encourage poor countries like Surinam and Gabon to sell off their natural resources. Often those in power locally and nationally see it as an easy way to get rich quick. Even the international banking system is not without blame in putting roads into forests to aid extraction without considering the environmental cost. To economists behind their desks in the United States and Europe it seems a good way for helping poor countries to "develop", even though such "development" is not sustainable.

The European Union is the second largest aid agency in the world. What they are doing in the name of development is sometimes disastrous, like the £48 million spent on the oil palm project in Nigeria which went ahead without any environmental assessment, and the £10 million road building project in Cameroon through forests and close to reserves, which was against the advice of the African Development Bank.

The Kayapo of Brazil have a 3 million hectare reserve to protect their way of life. They have been selling mahogany and have now joined the consumer society. In contrast the poor Bainings people of the mountains of Papua New Guinea have the courage to resist the bribes of Asian loggers who roam the countryside trying to bribe politicians to circumvent the law thus creating social disharmony.

The United Nations Convention on Environment and Development (UNCED) took place in Rio in 1992. This big conference, attended by heads of major governments, has produced very little. Even the gains made have been eroded. The proposal for a global forest convention was rejected in favour of a non legally binding statement of principle. The convention on biological diversity signed by 140 countries fared no better, and an attempt to introduce a forest protocol was resisted by most governments. The Commission on Sustainable Development (CSD) held a major meeting in 1995 but failed to get agreement for action. The International Tropical Timber Organisation (ITTO) came under pressure from non governmental organizations (NGOs) and set a target for all tropical timber being traded to come from sustainably managed forests by the year 2000. It has failed, and the WWF has said that many ongoing ITTO projects are really subsidized logging. Then in 1993 some tropical countries suggested expanding this proposal to include temperate timber as well, but immediately northern countries objected strongly – Why?

There are continual efforts being made to save the forests from total destruction but successful results are few and are overshadowed by the immense problems. One success worth mentioning is that of a small band of aboriginal people in the interior of British Columbia, Canada who have won protection for a 1,000 square kilometres of their ancestral wilderness from loggers.

FISHING

If anything could have a more serious effect on the environment and conservation than the destruction of forests, it is the horrendous damage being done to the marine environment. Over-fishing, the damaging methods used, pollution and soil washed onto coral reefs from soil erosion, all take their toll and seem to be unstoppable.

More and still more fish are being taken from the seas in spite of attempts at control. In 1950 the world catch of edible fish was 20 million tons. In 1990 it has risen to 100 million. But that's not the whole picture. An additional 27 million metric tons of unwanted marine life are caught and dumped overboard. One example is the weight of the "bycatch", as it's called, in shrimp fishing which is up to 800% more than the shrimps caught. This bycatch consists of large numbers of young fish, so fish stock can't replenish themselves.

The population of anchovies crashed and hasn't recovered. So has the herring and cod in some areas, and in other areas salmon. The population of the blue fin tuna – a delicacy in Japan – is now only 1% of its former population size, yet is still being fished. Some years ago attempts were made to ban the fishing of this species at the biennial meeting of the Conservation on International Trade in Endangered Species (CITES). Japan strongly opposed this proposal and it was dropped because an 8 foot (2½ metre) blue fin tuna would fetch US$75,000 in Japan. These fish are caught in the southern ocean using long lines that have up to 3,000 baited hooks on each line and stretch for miles behind the ship. The bait also attracts sea birds which are caught and killed. In 1991, 44,000 albatrosses were killed by the Japanese fleet. We simply don't know how many are killed by the fleets of South Korea, China, Taiwan, and Hawaii, South America and South Africa. What we do know is that the albatross is now a threatened species and may soon be extinct. The world may soon lose this magnificent bird with a 7ft wingspan and a life expectancy of almost as long as humans, and lose the blue fin tuna as well.

Worse still is the drift net, known by conservationists as a "wall of death". It was developed in Japan. The nets are long, up to 30 kilometres. One edge is kept near the surface of the sea by floats. The other edge is weighted so that the 10 metre deep net hangs vertically. It catches every creature that blunders against it, fish of course, but also turtles, whales, dolphins and sea birds.

The director general of UNESCO (United Nations Educational, Scientific and Cultural Organisation) launched the International Year of the Ocean in 1998 to focus the attention of people and governments on the importance of the marine environment for sustainable development. He doesn't say what he means by development, but goes on to mention increasing threats "of pollution, population pressure, over fishing and coastal zone degradation". If he means conservation, why use the word development? The world has lost half its coastal wetlands. Mangrove forests and seagrass beds have been destroyed, coral reefs are being pillaged and damaged and fisheries are in serious decline. According to the United Nations Food and Agricultural Organisation (FAO) nearly 70% of the world's marine fish are heavily or over exploited. In the major fishing areas productivity has fallen in the last few years and some areas report a drop of 30%. In 1995 the United Nations called fisheries globally non sustainable. Between 1970 and 1990 the world's fishing fleet doubled and now has twice the capacity to catch what is available. So as fishing became inefficient, subsidies in various forms totalling over US$50 billion have been made available to preserve employment. It would be better to spend the money on creating new jobs. For every million dollars of investment small-scale fisheries employ only a few thousand people, while industrial scale fisheries only employ less than ten people. One of the best fishing areas was the Canadian east coast fishery, worth some US$2 billion per annum. By 1989, the catch wasn't large enough to keep all the processing plants open. Scientists thought they could manage the fishery. They got it wrong. Drastic measures were proposed but the politicians refused to implement them.

The Black Sea is well on the way to becoming a dead sea. Catches have fallen ten fold and the number of commercially valuable species has dropped from 26 to 5. Romania dumps 170 million metric tons of raw sewage into the Black Sea and Turkey dumps some 500 million tons per annum. Between 40 and 50 million tons of raw sewage are discharged into the Mediterranean. Calcutta dumps 400 million metric tons into the ocean and Bombay dumps 365 million. With the best will in the world it would take many years to install treatment plants and there is neither will nor money. For example, the Oslo Dumping Convention and the London Dumping Convention, both endorsed in 1972, are not being enforced.

Fish farms, aquaculture, are likely to hasten the loss of habitat because they are a source of pollution by releasing excess food, faeces and disease. Fisheries suffer from habitat destruction as well as pollution. Two-thirds of the valuable fish spend their earlier lives in shallow coastal waters and because half the estuarine and salt marshes and mangrove forests have been destroyed, fewer fish are developing.

A lot of effort in the form of conventions has been put into tackling these problems. The Convention on the Law of the Sea was adopted in 1982 and entered into force in 1994, and it is strongly supported by most states. It has solved some problems relating to jurisdiction such as the 200-mile limit, but hasn't provided answers to the major problems outlined above. It created three institutions – The Commission on the Limits of the Continental Shelf, The International Sea Bed Authority (whose powers were not acceptable to major industrial countries including Britain and the USA), and The International Tribunal for the Law of the Sea (which handles disputes). The Tribunal established a general framework requesting states to adopt laws and standards, but there is still no action.

There are some small successes. The United States has established a protected marine area called The Florida Keys National Marine Sanctuary, which covers 2,700 square miles of ocean. A World Heritage site of some 12,000 square kilometres off the coast of Mauritania was created in 1976. Now however, the local people called Imraguen, who were allowed to fish for subsistence, have awoken to the international market and consumerism. They are killing sharks for shark fins and getting US$100 per kilo for the Asian market. It is not a sustainable fishery because of the shark's long reproductive cycle and it will soon crash.

Freshwater fish are not immune from these problems. Not only are fish stocks being depleted but many lakes are dying due to pollution. For example, the Canadian Department of Fisheries has said that 14,000 lakes in Canada are dead and many others are dying, mainly due to acid rain. Not only is this source of food declining but the effects on bio-diversity are incalculable.

CONTROL OF DISEASE

In spite of all the concern expressed at conferences, symposia and in the media, in spite of all the resolutions passed to conserve the

© Colin Seddon

Badgers are being killed in parts of Britain as it is believed they spread TB to cattle

natural environment, when push comes to shove, profits always take precedence. Even though there may be other ways of reaching the same or similar ends which may take longer and are less profitable, with less harm to the environment, they will not easily be considered. Draconian measures are often taken to control diseases and pests that affect profits. Pesticides have already been mentioned. No one knows the long term effect on bio-diversity and few seem to care. A simple example is the use of a product which kills the parasites of cattle and sheep in Africa. It persists in the animal's faeces and kills free living insects like the dung beetle, which is an important link in the regeneration of trees. This beetle lays its eggs in dung which it then buries a foot or so underground, together with the undigested seeds of trees. Without the efforts of these beetles, the seeds cannot germinate and grow.

The attempts to stop the spread of disease from wildlife to domestic animals often have dire consequences, while the risk of spreading from domestic animals to wildlife is ignored. In Britain the government has ordered the killing of badgers in certain areas because it believes they spread TB to cattle. The possibility that cattle may spread TB to badgers, or more likely that there may be an overall factor responsible for the spread of TB in both cattle and badgers, is ignored.

In Canada, both tuberculosis and brucellosis were passed from cattle to bison. The solution proposed was the removal and destruction of bison. In America's Yellowstone National Park, bison contracted brucellosis from cattle. It seems that agricultural bureaucracies have a free hand to destroy the very basis of wildlife and nature conservation in the name of disease control.

Perhaps the worst case that has come to light is the death of thousands of wild animals caused by fences erected to keep cattle free of foot and mouth disease in Botswana. The story is rather curious. Botswana is the size of Texas and situated in the arid Kalahari region of Southern Africa. Its 1½ million inhabitants are not poor, for Botswana has the highest GNP of any African country. It is rich in diamonds and it used to be rich in wildlife. A study in 1990 revealed that the central Kalahari has lost 99% of its wildebeest and 95% of its hartebeest in the previous decade. Once these animals were so numerous that they equalled the great herds of the Serengeti. Now they have to be protected. The cause of the decline is due to a lack of understanding of the ecology, and the misguided aid from the EEC and the World Bank. Several fences hundreds of miles long were constructed. In one year alone (1983) about 50,000 wildebeest died along the Kuke fence. Subsequently many more zebra and wildebeest died along the fence which was constructed in the Nata region in 1990. Can one assume that this shows an inability to learn? Was it the enthusiasm for democracy, or the hatred and fear of communism, that encouraged the West to bolster Botswana's economy and the ruling elite? Cattle ranching, the traditional business of the people, became more commercialized and centralized in the hands of about 5,000 rich farmers, many of whom were government officials. They received large loans from the World Bank (US$1.65 million from the USA in 1972), to spread giant ranches into the fragile marginal lands which is the traditional home of wildlife. Despite Botswana's defaulting on repayment the World Bank approved a further loan of US$10 million to create more ranches.

To maximize the profits the beasts had to be exported to whoever could pay the most. The European community agreed to take about 19,000 tons of beef annually under specially favoured trading arrangements which were 40% above the world market prices, according to a letter received from the Director of Veterinary Services. Two-thirds of the revenue goes to between 2 and 3% of cattle owners. But the beef doesn't stay in Europe. Much is re-exported to countries such as Hong Kong and some is given away to Angola. Under the LOME Convention in 1975 the EC buys 80% of Botswana's beef. There is, however, one reservation namely the beef must be free of foot and mouth disease, a disease that has been almost eliminated from Europe. As usual, wildlife is blamed as being a reservoir of diseases which can be passed on to domestic animals and humans, such as tuberculosis in badgers which can infect cows. But it rarely happens, partly because there is little contact between wild and domestic animals, and diseases in wild animals are naturally self limiting, i.e., the affected animal either recovers, is killed by a predator or dies. Diseases usually spread from domestic to wild animals. I suppose when one doesn't know the source of the disease it is better to blame wildlife and to be seen to be actively involved in preventing any possible spread than to shake one's head and do nothing, especially if one's job may be at stake. So this prevention entailed the construction of some 3,000 miles of fences criss-crossing the country. These long fences interrupted the normal migration routes of wildlife in search of water and new pastures as the seasons changed. Many thousands of cattle died against the fences from starvation and thirst.

The beef subsidy encouraged the number of cattle in Botswana to increase to 3.5 million, which is twice as many as the human population. Instead of benefiting large numbers of people it made 2% of the human population very rich. Many believe that this large number of cattle is above the carrying capacity of the country and is causing environmental damage.

The future of wildlife in Botswana looks bleak. Once wild herds of some 3 million are now reduced to under 1 million and may soon disappear altogether. The Kalahari could be reduced to a wasteland of shifting sand, and this scenario is already apparent around the cattle posts and water points.

To compound the damage to wildlife, poaching is rife and uncontrolled and takes place openly. Hunting, with or without licences, is extensive. The irony is that if all the fences were removed the wildlife would suffer from uncontrolled invasion of cattle. By far the main threat to wildlife is greed disguised in platitudes. Stewardship for nature's bounty has been replaced by exploitation in the name of development and jobs.

Vaccination of wildlife to stop the spread of disease has a down side in that disease is part of natural selection, which for aeons of time has ensured that the fittest survive. Vaccination interferes with natural selection and unless carried out year after year, can create a susceptible population. It is argued that disease introduced by human activities such as canine distemper in lions contracted from domestic dogs, could and should be controlled by vaccination. However, this will interfere with natural selection. After all, nature has coped and no species has become extinct because of disease. In any case it is doubtful if humans can ever control their domestic animals in ways to prevent the spread of diseases to wildlife. An example of how nature copes is when the European harbour seal became infected with a variant of canine distemper and over half of the North Sea population died. The disease ran its course and the population is increasing in numbers again.

ATTITUDE TO ANIMALS

The prevalent attitude to animals is to regard them simply as items of trade and not as sentient beings. When the General Agreement on

Culling in South Africa has left its remaining elephant herds with high incidences of stress-related diseases

Tariffs and Trade (GATT) was worked out and signed, the World Trade Organisation (WTO) was established to resolve any arguments or disagreements that might arise. The popular will was disregarded, public health risks and moral considerations such as the use of child labour and the suffering of animals were ruled inadmissible as arguments against trade. So laws protecting human health, the environment and animals were swept away. For example, when the United States placed an embargo on tuna caught by a method which also killed thousands of dolphins which were then dumped overboard as trash, it was denounced by Mexico as a barrier to trade and the WTO successfully sued the US government. The law designed to protect dolphins was declared illegal by WTO.

In the name of trade most of the laws of western governments have enacted to protect the environment and public health and animals are being swept away one by one.

Whenever there is money to be made from animals there are people who either have no scruples or are totally indifferent to animals suffering. Daphne Sheldrick is very concerned by the proposal to train elephants to carry tourists on safari. Elephants have been trained for several hundred years for war, ceremonial occasions and logging. Yet relatively few people know the cruelty inflicted in the process.

When training of elephants in Kenya was recently proposed by an entrepreneur, Daphne wrote:

> This country has always enjoyed a gentler approach to wildlife conservation than is practised in Southern Africa, sensitive to the welfare of animals and mindful also that animals, like

> people, should be allowed to live in peace and enjoy a quality of life. Kenya was the first to ban hunting, the first to burn its ivory, the one country to accept natural controls on elephant populations as a safer and better option than intrusive interference that would trigger the run-away train of raw commercialism that clouds judgement, as we have seen so often in South Africa. There, they are now beginning to reap what they have sown – traumatized populations with a high incidence of diseases such as TB where harassment and stress have been a contributory factor; a very smutty image over the cruelty of their culling and capture operations, and an even smuttier image internationally because of their "training" tactics in relation to the Tuli calves, snatched from their living families and brutalized in the most hideous fashion to make them compliant for circuses, zoos and, in fact, Elephant Back Safaris. Why do we have to tarnish our compassionate image by now embarking on the introduction of something which must inevitably involve a degree of cruelty when dealing with such powerful animals, irrespective of how gently this is done?

The proposal is that wild caught elephant would never be contemplated. They would use only African elephants brought back from the United States, and offer them a better quality of life in Africa. Nor would these be ex circus or zoo elephants but all would be elephants that have been born on ranches in the US and which have never been subjected to cruelty. But how can anyone be sure that this can be controlled once this pioneer operation has proved commercially lucrative, as it surely will. We have seen the pitfalls of opening something that cannot be controlled due to vested interests with the bushmeat trade that now threatens the extinction of "meat species" in many places. We have seen the flagrant disregard for the law in the rape of the Karura Forest and other hardwood forests, and numerous other instances of flouting or bending the rules, because big money is involved. Where there is money to be made, corruption creeps in, and when corruption is practised by people in positions of power, there is very little that can halt it, as we have seen time and time again in this country. Can we risk exposing live elephants to what is, after all, yet another form of trade, and is it wise to open this Pandora's Box that may never be able to be controlled or closed? There is great wisdom in never taking the first step if the repercussions of making that step are so obviously fraught with pitfalls.

And will other operators in a hurry for "the mighty dollar" go to the trouble of identifying "friendly" African elephants held overseas, and then incur the expense of bringing them back to Kenya? Of course not. It will be much easier to get them here, especially now that South African expertise is readily available, both for the capture and brutal "training". Yet again, calves will be abducted from their families and brutally dominated into submission in order to affect a quick sale. The Tuli case is a glaring example of the suffering that monetary greed can lead to. As a court case, brought by the National Society for the Prevention of Cruelty to Animals (NSPCA), continued through the South African courts, many of the elephants were forced to remain at the animal trader's facility. Even though the NSPCA were given monitoring rights over the handling of the abused calves they were not allowed to move them from the facility and a year after their capture the brutality and beatings continued. If anything, they were far worse than before. However, a High Court injunction was in place to prevent the facts becoming public.

Furthermore, removing the elephants from the wild for sale to safari parks or elephant backed safaris was condoned by conservation organizations such as the Rhino and Elephant Foundation and the World Wildlife Fund as a valid form of utilizing "surplus" elephants. In a position statement released on 2 October 1998, shortly before the NSPCA was granted a court order to seize the elephants, "to prevent further suffering", WWF South Africa said, "In fact, we applaud the private reserve owners in this area for tackling the elephant overpopulation problem by the only means available to them . . ." They went on to say, "our appraisal of the current operation is that there is no more cruelty involved with this operation than there is in many relocation operations of previously wild, free-ranging dangerous animals."

The training for elephant under safaris of an ex-crop raiding Indian elephant has similarly fallen beneath the international spotlight. Unhappily, domestication of elephants and cruelty are synonymous. Attempts to domesticate the African elephant, whether for circuses, zoos, or elephant back-riding, have not benefited the elephant as a species in any way at all, but only led to frustration, abuse and suffering. The African elephant is a much more volatile animal than its Asian cousin and tragedies as a result of captive elephants going berserk are legendary. The genetic memory, known as "instinct", is frustrated once an elephant is captive, irrespective of its treatment, and this invariably breeds resentment in the elephant psyche. Like humans, personality also plays a large part; not all elephants are alike, some being more manageable than others. But no frustrated elephant can ever be truly trusted.

And why should Africa be a dumping ground for the world's elephant victims of captivity, most of whom will be psychotic to a greater or lesser extent, because they have been frustrated from fulfilling their natural role within the environment and prevented by humans from leading a normal wild life amongst their own kind? Elephants are highly social animals that need the contact of their family and kin. Why should these abused elephants be sent back to Africa simply because they have become unmanageable, whilst a fresh batch of normal calves are imported, from whom their owners can reap rich rewards until they too turn psychotic and dangerous? Is this not just another form of trade in live animals, plundering sane babies from Africa and returning the "used goods"?

Many elephants held overseas apparently suffer from diseases such as herpes, the subject of an extensive article in the press recently. Would not bringing back elephants held in other countries risk the introduction of diseases into our resident populations?

The proposal is that there would be criteria drawn up by a panel of experts which would lay down the guidelines for the handling of elephants. There would be experts on the board to monitor what goes on and experts from overseas to oversee the training and that Dr Leakey will ensure that Kenya Wildlife Service (KWS) never slips back retrogressively.

But Dr Leakey will not be around forever, and no one can guarantee or predict the direction KWS will take under future management. No amount of controls will be binding if a director feels like changing the ground rules, so any criteria laid down for the treatment of captive elephants will only be as good as the paper on which it is written.

Stringent criteria governing the conduct of scientists in a national park were drawn up and approved by the Board of Trustees way back in the 1960s, but these have long been ignored. Using the cover of science, some national parks have breached existing laws. There have been cases when guidelines governing the conduct of scientists in national parks have been approved but have subsequently been ingnored, and wardens appear powerless to intervene or simply choose to turn a blind eye. Criteria are meaningless if the "powers that be" choose to disregard them.

The orphan elephants at Daphne Sheldrick's nursery are rehabilitated and eventually return to the wild of their own free will

And the overseas "experts"? Who are they and what are their credentials? How can a foreigner who has never been exposed to wild elephant populations, and who has only handled frustrated captives, be an elephant "expert"?

And who, Daphne Sheldrick asks, will benefit from the introduction of Elephant Back Safaris? The answer must surely be only a few wealthy operators, at the expense of exposing the African handlers to danger on a daily basis. Should one of the riding elephants be in season and be approached by a musth bull, is the wild elephant going to be shot because it poses a danger to a tourist rider? Or are the wild elephants going to be driven away by thunder flashes ahead of the riders, as was suggested by the Laikipia Forum, and if so, why should wild elephants be subjected to yet another form of harassment? How can an elephant differentiate between gunfire from poaching, shot in croplands and sudden thunderflashes in the park, which is supposed to be their one refuge? Because of the degree of harassment that will be necessary in the interests of tourist safety, presumably Elephant Back Riding could not work in a national park, so it will happen on private land where there will be even less control on standards.

There have always been laws governing what could and could not be done in our national parks, but we have constantly seen the ground rules change. Nowadays night driving is permitted, with animals dazzled by spotlights, in the hope of showing a tourist a kill. Off road driving is condoned to the detriment of the habitat; it leaves scars that last for years on fragile landscapes. Domestic animals such as camels, have been introduced into national parks, yet it used to be illegal to introduce domestic animals into a national park. Nowadays cattle compete openly for both water and grazing in the parks, whereas previously this was under control.

"Training" an elephant by the reward method might be feasible (until the elephant doesn't feel like doing what it is told) but it will also result in potential "problem animals" who, should they break free of their restraining chains, will immediately seek "rewards" around human habitation elsewhere and end up being shot. It is for this reason that no rewards of any sort are ever given by hand to orphans, for elephants quickly become addicted to junk food and inevitably end up a menace around human settlement. Once again, it is the local people who will suffer.

There is nothing educational in seeing a captive elephant in chains near any school. What is educational is allowing children and the public access to needy orphans in Kenya's elephant nursery, and providing each and every one with information about why elephants should not be domesticated and utilized for commercial gain. Kenya's orphaned elephants are world famous and the fact that they are ultimately returned to the wild successfully is a world first. They are leaders in elephant management and elephant welfare. It will be a sad day indeed when this image is tarnished, as tarnished it will be, once the commercial exploitation of elephants is condoned in Kenya.

Returning a captive elephant to Africa, and exposing it again to the wild situation that remains imprinted in its genetic memory, and then denying it the freedom of expression, is, in my opinion, yet another form of cruelty that we cannot measure but is sure to have repercussions.

In conclusion, the welfare of wild animals has definitely not improved and the day that Kenya condones the attempted domestication of the African elephant would be a sad one indeed. Let us not expose elephants to what, with hindsight, has done them no favours whatsoever but which opens the door to abuse. From Elephant Back Riding will come "Green Hunting from an Elephant", perhaps even bow and arrow hunts from the back of an elephant, the implanting of microchips so that a bored and curious global public can trace their movement on the Internet, etc. The tide of Southern African commercialism creeping into our wildlife policies is, to me, deeply disturbing, when the wisdom of caution has always stood us in such good stead during the most difficult eras.

The elephant is a noble and majestic animal and it is at its best in the wild, living according to the laws of nature, and fulfilling the functions for which it has evolved. A domesticated elephant is a tragic replica of the real thing. Let us keep our elephants in the wild?

RELIGION

The second major problem which must be reversed is the decline into a materialistic non-religious culture – a Godless age.

"The world is fragile, handle it with prayer" was graffiti on a London tube station wall 20 years ago. It is even more true now when today's religion seems to be technology and the priests are men in white coats.

It has been claimed that the Christian religion preaches man's domination and exploitation of nature. In the book of Genesis 1:28 we are told "Be fruitful and multiply and replenish the earth and subdue it; have dominion over the fish of the sea and over the fowl of the air."

That seems clear enough, yet the real message of the Bible is for humans to care for the world as expressed in Genesis 2:15: "and the Lord took the man and put him in the Garden of Eden to dress it and to keep it". The phrase "be fruitful and multiply" applied to the period when the Jews were exiled and the prophets were trying to keep up their morale.

Judaism also preaches care and reverence for nature. The key Talmudic principle is, "See my works, see their beauty, their perfection. Everything I have created I have created for you. Take care not to spoil or destroy my world because there will be no one to mend it after you."

The Islamic approach to man and nature is set within four principles, namely, Tawheed, Fitra, Mizan and Khalifa. In God's plan, humans are guardians of the Earth because of their ability to reason. "It is He who has appointed you as viceroys of the Earth" (Qur'an, 6.165).

The Buddhist teaching is the middle way and reverence for life. Mander Hindus are taught to "See God in all things, behind all forms, behind all names. There is not a grain of earth that is devoid of God". In what is probably one of the most beautiful and profound statements on the environment ever made, the American Indian Chief Seattle said in 1854:

> Teach your children what we have taught our children that the earth is our mother

And of God he said:

> The earth is precious to Him and to harm the earth is to heap contempt on its creator.

Probably all native beliefs, from American Indians to African Bushmen and the Australian Aboriginals, ascribe a spiritual significance to nature.

We have lost much of our feeling of care and protection of nature in a few decades. Yet deep down our emotions retain a faint reverence for life, especially when unencumbered by modern trappings we regard the sea, the sky, the mountains and the forests.

PACE OF LIFE

"Speed," says David Orr in an article in Resurgence, "is one of the major problems of modern life."[19] Quick returns and rapid growth dominate the global economy. He compares our life today to the affects of doubling the speed of water, which increases the size of soil particles it carries by 64 times, and does not recharge the aquifers. Humans have drained wetlands allowing water to flow faster and thereby cause flooding. He describes how the increasing speed of living has changed many things. Before the war, groceries, milk, meat and bread were all delivered to one's home. But now people have to drive to the supermarkets. In many towns, money doesn't stay in the local economy for long, so there is no multiplier effect such as there used to be, and still is, in the Amish communities in the United States, who grow their own food. They use horsepower and make many of the necessities of life for themselves. The Amish are kept at the pace of the horse which they use in farming and distribution. The capital of the Amish farm is in buildings and land, and not in machinery. The pace of life is slow and rewarding.

Now we have computers to speed up office work, and the Internet which provides so much useless superficial information that people are drowning in it. Information and knowledge are not the same. Wisdom is being lost.

Roads are widened, motorways are built to increase the speed of traffic, but for what purpose? As David Orr points out, "We can never conserve biotic resources nor build a sustainable civilization that operates at the present velocity". We must take time to make things that are durable and repairable. We must slow the speed of living.

One thing is certain, we cannot reject science, which is needed to take us back from the brink provided we recognize that it is not value free and does not hold a monopoly of the truth. Science just needs to be more holistic in its approach and accept that conservation should not depend entirely on human benefit. Some say that science is determined by culture and social values. Others argue that science is objective. Industries want to gather evidence that they cause no damage. Environmentalists point out that there is much less money to investigate a full range of their affects on nature. Disputes between scientists about the facts of pollution confirm that there are no really objective facts. Science cannot help us decide values, and only in that sense is it value free, but not in the sense of providing objective knowledge. Scientific theories spring from all sorts of values. It is because of this that science needs to tackle the almost insurmountable problems of today.

Niles Eldridge, in his book called *Dominions*,[12] points out that from about 1.7 million years ago, armed with fire and tools, our ancestors spread across the world and wherever they went large mammals disappeared. Then 10,000 years ago, when agriculture was established, humans became disengaged from nature and plundered and polluted the bounty they regarded as their own. Eldridge believes that the solution is human population control.

Richard Leakey and Roger Lewins, in their book *The Sixth Extinction*,[13] propose that it is human beings that are causing the sixth extinction, which is inevitable unless we change our approach to nature and our attitude about our place on Planet Earth. It is this change in our attitude to nature, from one of exploitation to one of caring and controlling our numbers, that are the basic needs. There is still time, but not much.

Notes

1. N. Myers, *The Sinking Ark*. Pergamon Press, 1979.
2. E. O. Wilson, *In Search of Nature*. Penguin, 1998.
3. D. Suzuki, *Inventing the Future*. Allen & Unwin, 1990.
4. J. Jacobson, "Homeless near a thousand homes". *People*, vol. 17, no. 1, 1990.
5. N. Myers, "Consuming the Future". *People and the Planet*, vol. 8, no. 1, 1999.

6. R. Carson, *Silent Spring*. Fawcett, 1962.
7. Y. Havel, "Spirit of the Earth". Resurgence, no. 191, 1998.
8. A. Maslow, *Motivation and Personality*. Harper & Row, 1970.
9. J. E. Cummins, "PCB's: Can the world's sea mammals survive them". *The Ecologist*, vol. 28, p. 262, 1998.
10. H. Geist, "In tobacco control", cited in "Where there's smoke" by M Day. *New Scientist*, vol. 162, no. 2188.
11. David Orr, *Speed Resurgence*, no. 192, 1999.
12. N. Eldridge. *Dominion*. Henry Holt & Co., 1995.
13. R. Leakey and R. Lewins. *The Sixth Extinction*. Weidenfeld & Nicolson, 1995.

2 Can Economics be Green?

Lindsey Gillson

Many people believe that wildlife should pay its own way. They argue that revenue generated from wildlife can be used to fund conservation and that economic principles should guide conservation policy. However, creating commercial value for animals exposes them to market forces and has caused the demise of many wild animals. Ignoring economics analysis would be unrealistic in today's world, but economics are just one element in a more complex picture. This chapter explores some basic economic principles and discusses the implications for wildlife.

Many people believe that wildlife should pay its own way. They argue that revenue generated from wildlife can be used to fund conservation and that economic principles should guide conservation policy. However, there are some fundamental problems in applying economic principles to natural systems.

Market economics are explained in terms of supply and demand. Consumers demand more of a product when its price is low. Suppliers make more of a product when its price is high. Goods which are scarce are worth more because consumers are prepared to pay for more of them. If a product is too freely available, then consumers will not pay much for it and its price will be low. In a competitive free market, the price at which a product is sold depends on the balance between supply and demand. This balance is called the market equilibrium. It is reached as a result of individual suppliers and consumers pursuing the best financial option.

The famous economist Adam Smith has likened market forces to an "invisible hand".[1] When demand for a product increases, prices

The supply curve shows how the costs of supply vary with the amount produced. The demand curve shows how the quantity demanded varies with the price of the goods produced. The market equilibrium is the point at which the two curves intersect

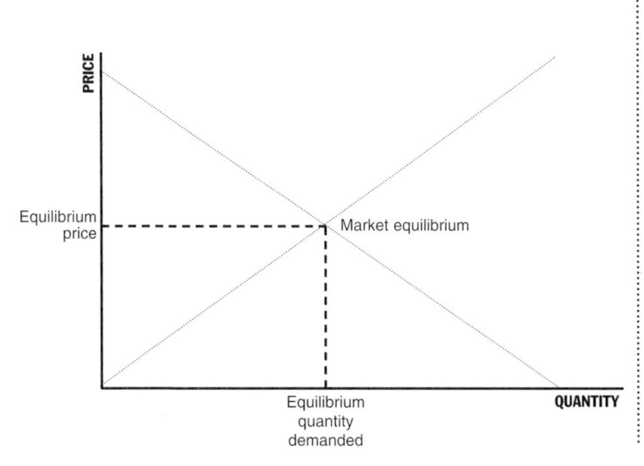

Figure: 2.1: The market model of supply and demand

also increase and manufacturers and retailers increase the supply of the product in response. Conversely, when demand for a product falls, prices drop and manufacturers and retailers cut back on the supply. A shortfall in the supply of a product will tend to drive prices up and stimulate increased production. Suppliers can stimulate demand, for example by advertising. Consumers can influence suppliers by their spending preferences; a consumer boycott can reduce demand to such an extent that it is no longer economic for a supplier to manufacture goods.

Renewable natural resources, such as trees or wild animal populations, are those that can grow and replace themselves. The rate at which replacement occurs is determined by environmental factors, such as climate and availability of food, as well as biological factors such as the life span of the harvested species and the number of offspring. The following discussion refers specifically to the lethal use of wildlife. This means that whole plants and animals must be killed in order to harvest the commercially valuable product. It contrasts with the non-consumptive use of natural resources, such as photographic tourism, which does not involve the death of plants or animals.

For wildlife, market forces can be a death trap. Unlike manufactured goods, the supply of wildlife cannot be adjusted to suit consumer whims. The rate of reproduction of animals and plants has intrinsic biological limits, which cannot be exceeded. Biological factors such as the gestation period are fixed and cannot be decreased in response to increased harvesting. The rate of increase of a population (recruitment) depends on the difference between birth rate and death rate; this is influenced by unpredictable factors such as food supply, weather conditions, rainfall and disease.

Once the demand for a wildlife product exceeds the rate of recruitment to the population, depletion of the population is inevitable. Long-lived species with low reproductive rates are especially vulner-

Fig. 2.2: The backward-bending supply curve for a harvested renewable resource

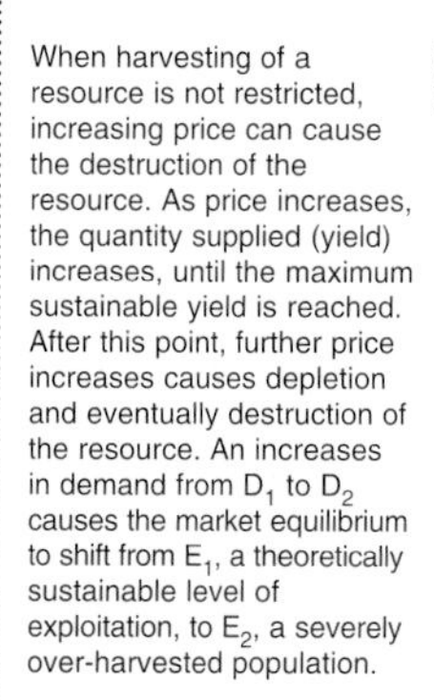
When harvesting of a resource is not restricted, increasing price can cause the destruction of the resource. As price increases, the quantity supplied (yield) increases, until the maximum sustainable yield is reached. After this point, further price increases causes depletion and eventually destruction of the resource. An increases in demand from D_1 to D_2 causes the market equilibrium to shift from E_1, a theoretically sustainable level of exploitation, to E_2, a severely over-harvested population.

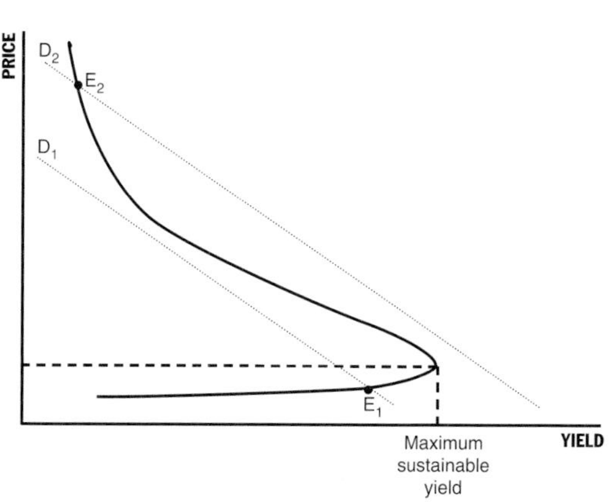

Many tiger body parts are used in traditional Chinese medicine. There is little or no evidence of their healing properties

able to over-harvesting. Instead of increasing in response to demand, the supply curve for over-harvested wildlife therefore bends backwards.[2] This indicates a reduced yield in response to increased demand. This situation is the opposite of what happens for manufactured commodities and explains the collapse of fish stocks in response to increasing harvesting effort.[3]

To make matters worse, the value of a wildlife product often becomes greater the more rare the species is. Collectors compete for what may be the last ever chance to buy. Connoisseurs revel in their exclusive purchases. The result, therefore, of the endangerment of a species can often be an increase in demand, and an increase in value. An example of this would be the use of rhino horn for ceremonial dagger handles and aphrodisiacs. The value of rhino horn has increased dramatically as rhino populations approach extinction.

At this point, trade restrictions may be introduced in an attempt to prevent the imminent extinction of the species. But as long as demand remains, this further restriction on supply simply leads to yet more increases in the price. If the financial gains are high enough or when poverty is bad enough, then this high value will create incentive for poaching and illegal trading. This occurred during the 1980s, when ivory quotas were imposed. The restriction in supply drove prices up. It was only a complete ban on the international trade in ivory, imposed with the support of most consumer nations, which allowed the control of poaching and the stabilization of most elephant populations.

Alternatives to many wildlife products are available. However, synthetic or non-endangered products may lack kudos or cultural importance. Rhino horn, for example, is made from a protein called keratin, the same substance of which human hair and nails are composed. Some pharmacists have said that it has no effect on the human body; its mythical aphrodisiac qualities are based on symbolism rather than any biological reality. Similarly, many healing and aphrodisiac qualities are attributed to tiger bone, but in fact its only affect on the human body is to act as a mild analgesic. A synthetic alternative to bear bile has been produced, yet bears are still hunted for their gall bladders or endure pain and suffering in bear farms. These examples illustrate the importance of cultural acceptance in changing the patterns of consumption of wildlife products.

THE EXTINCTION VORTEX

The higher the rate of harvesting of a wild population, the more likely is the depletion of that population. Small populations are vulnerable to inbreeding depression; a lack of genetic variability in small populations may increase the chance that genetic abnormalities will be exposed, making the population less "fit" or able to survive. Genetically homogeneous populations are also likely to be less able to adapt to new conditions, such as changing climate or the introduction of a disease.

Depleted populations of animals can enter what is known as the extinction vortex; once their population falls below a critical level, numbers start to plummet and the population has little or no chance of recovery. This phenomenon is known as "The Allee effect".[4] The effect may occur because, for example, social structures become disrupted and it becomes increasingly difficult for animals to find a mate. There are so few blue whales left, for example, that there is very little chance of fertile males and females finding one another.

THE DISCOUNT RATE, OPPORTUNITY COSTS AND THE FATE OF WILDLIFE

If conservation is evaluated within the conventional economic framework, then wildlife conservation must compete against alternative investment opportunities. This type of evaluation of wildlife could spell doom for many species.

The "opportunity cost" of a particular activity is a measure of the net benefits foregone by choosing that activity instead of an alternative one. For example, the opportunity cost of conserving wildlife habitat could be discussed in terms of the profits that could have been made by using the land for agriculture.[5] The opportunity cost of conserving wildlife on fertile land, which could be used for agriculture, is higher than that of conserving wildlife on land which is too dry or poor for other purposes.

The longer you wait to spend a given amount of money, the less it is worth; £5 in 1970 would buy far more than £5 today. The rate at which the value of money decreases over time is called the discount rate. It is equivalent to the interest rate, which is the term used when the value of money increases over time. The discount rate is the opportunity cost of investing in capital assets, rather than keeping a sum of money in the bank.

The discount rate and the opportunity cost are important when investors are deciding how best to spend their money. If, as the "wise-use" movement would have us believe, animals must pay their way, then those species which have a low reproductive rate are doomed by economics. The rate of growth of large mammals like elephants and whales is low – perhaps less than 5%. If the interest rate is higher than this, or other investment opportunities are available which give a higher return, then economics dictates that an investor should harvest the population to extinction, (or at least until further harvesting became impractical).[6] The income from this one-off harvest would then be more profitably invested elsewhere. We should therefore be very wary of those who claim that harvesting elephants for ivory is the best way to ensure their future. This phenomenon also explains the economic causes of the over-harvesting of mahogany.[7]

For open access resources, where harvesting is a free for all, the discount rate is infinite, because harvesters do not place any value on future profit, only on what can be made now. Harvesters do not gain by harvesting at a low level, because other harvesters will simply take what is left. The future value of the resource is zero and there is no economic incentive for harvesters to conserve it.

When a high level of investment is needed in order to begin the harvesting operation, the pressure to make profit is still greater. For example, the millions required to purchase and equip a commercial whaling vessel must be recouped before any profit is made by the whaling company. The pressure to generate revenue is thus completely dissociated from the biological parameters governing the whale population. Once an industry is established and dependent on a fixed supply of a natural resource, harvesting is likely to continue relentlessly until the resource is destroyed; witness the demise of many of the world's fisheries and whale populations.

USE IT OR LOSE IT?

It is argued that creating an economic value for species will ensure that revenue is available for conservation. But the preceding discussion has shown how economic principles can create the incentive for over-exploitation, one of the major causes of extinction. Furthermore, some species are threatened as a direct result of their economic worth. The "use it or lose it" argument simply does not work in reality. Use of wildlife creates incentives for over-harvesting and poaching and ensures that vast amounts of money must be spent on anti-poaching, simply to retain the status quo. Costly conservation measures are

Tigers are at the brink of extinction because of the economic value of their bones

required directly because market forces would lead to overexploitation and depletion. Species like tiger and rhino, which have a commercial value, require intensive anti-poaching measures to protect them.

A further danger of the "use it or lose it" rationale is that many species are not commercially utilized by humans. In fact, the proportion of species that are used for commercial purposes is very small. If wildlife has to pay to stay, then are the millions of "worthless" species doomed to extinction? We do not even know how many species there are in the world; estimates range from ten million to thirty million. It would obviously be impossible to create an economic value for all of them.

Humans are entirely dependent on a vast range of species, which have no commercial value whatsoever. Entire ecosystems, not commercially valuable species, are responsible for maintaining the water and air on which our existence depends.

Even where an economic value has been created for species, there is no guarantee that the species, or the range state will receive any benefit. Equity remains a serious problem and further undermines the "pay to stay" theory. For example, in Latin America, residents hold only 11% of biotechnology patents; the remainder are held by corporations from developed countries.[8] Simply creating a commercial value for wildlife does not guarantee an incentive for range states to conserve natural resources. Placing economic value at the heart of conservation can provide a convenient cover for profiteering by those countries with the means to extract, transport and market goods.

There is no guarantee that species with an economic value will survive in the long term. The qualities valued by humans change over time. Many traditional breeds of livestock and crops have been replaced by modern varieties and are now in danger of extinction. If their survival depended entirely on their commercial value, they would disappear completely, because they are no longer considered economically valuable. Nevertheless, such breeds constitute an important genetic resource and possess qualities of hardiness, resistance and adaptability, which have been lost from modern varieties. Groups like the Rare Breeds Trust (for animals) and the Henry Doubleday Institute (for crops) are dedicated to their protection.

As the human population grows, the area of land available to wildlife is decreasing and there is increasing conflict between man and wildlife. This has led to the argument that unless a monetary value is created for wildlife, its presence will not be tolerated. Many cultures have coexisted with other species for many thousands of years, regardless of whether the other species had any economic or even utilitarian value. It is our modern economic systems that must bear at least part of the responsibility for creating conflict between man and other animals. If conservation funds were not absorbed into anti-poaching work and security measures, then perhaps more resources would be available for conflict reduction.

Over-exploitation is one of the major threats to wildlife, along with habitat loss. Species that have no commercial value are not as likely to be over-exploited. Therefore, while there may be no commercial incentives for the protection of the vast majority of the world's species, there is also no incentive for their over-exploitation. Exploitation for commercial gain has driven tigers, rhinos and many species of whales to the brink of extinction.

ECONOMIES OF SCALE AND THE LAW OF SPECIALIZATION

Uniform, mass-produced goods can be made and sold more cheaply than hand-crafted, unique ones. This is called an economy of scale, which means that larger scale businesses are generally more competitive than small ones. For renewable natural resources, the cost per animal, fish, or tree harvested generally declines the bigger the harvest is. This is because cost-saving technology, like larger fishing vessels, can be introduced for larger scale operations.

One of the consequences of economies of scale is that businesses tend to be at their most efficient when they concentrate all of their efforts on just one or a few products. Economic productivity is highest when diversity is lowest; this is the principle of specialization.[9] In terms of crops, for example, economies of scale and the principle of specialization have dictated that intensively managed monocultures are the most efficient means of production. This intensive form of agriculture is often locally inappropriate and environmentally damaging.

In economic terms, "wildlands" can be defined as those areas that have not been substantially modified by the force of specialization.[10]

Under this definition, "wildlife" can be defined as all of the existing and potential goods and services flowing from such wildlands.

The law of specialization has dangerous implications for the harvesting of wild populations of animals. If wild areas come to be considered simply as a source of resources, then increasingly intensive management is inevitable. Ecosystems will be manipulated in order to favour those species that yield the most valuable product for humans. An example would be the reduction of predator populations, if prey species were being harvested. Such manipulation could be disastrous in terms of the long-term survival of ecosystems.

For example, during the 17th and 18th centuries, the cape fur seal was over-exploited. Its population has recovered in the 20th century due to conservation measures. It was expected that the increase in seal numbers would have a deleterious effect on stocks of commercially valuable hake (*Merluccius capensis* and *M. paradoxus*). Culling of seals was suggested in order to prevent this. In fact, population models predicted that culling of seals would actually decrease hake stocks. This is because *M. capensis* feeds on *M. paradoxus*. Culling seals would actually increase the pressure on *M. paradoxus*, resulting in a net loss of hake biomass.[11] The attempt to reduce predation by seal culling would have had disastrous consequences, because of an incomplete understanding of ecosystem interactions.

Similarly, in some national parks in Africa, elephant populations are controlled by culling in order to protect tree cover. However, Acacia, which are one of the most important savannah trees, cannot regenerate under their own canopy.[12] It could be that elephants are actually promoting the regeneration of tree cover, by creating spaces in which young trees can become established. Preventing the removal of mature trees by elephants might depress regeneration and therefore threaten tree cover in the long term.

Human aims for ecosystems are often relatively short term and are based around aesthetic judgements, which differ between individuals or over time. Ecosystems are complicated and our understanding of them is incomplete. The economic framework cannot deal adequately with the complexities and uncertainties of ecology.

Taken to its extreme, the law of specialization will favour economically valuable species to the exclusion of all others. Economically speaking, plantations are more efficient than natural forests and game ranches more efficient than savannah ecosystems. An example would be the proliferation of ostrich farms during the early nineties, many of which are now bankrupt.

Specialization in agriculture has led to intensification, reduced genetic diversity, animal welfare problems, pollution, homogeneity, and lack of adaptation to local conditions. There are also health risks to human consumers, such as salmonella and BSE, which are a direct result of intensive farming methods.

Experience has shown that it is not enough simply to create

economic value for species. The free market should not be entrusted with the future survival of species.

COST-BENEFIT ANALYSIS

Economic analysis, by its very nature, focuses on cash value and does not have adequate mechanisms to evaluate other worth. The over-emphasis on economic analysis has focused attention on species which humans use, or which are in danger of extinction. The whole picture of complex interdependent ecosystems is not addressed.

Cost-benefit analysis is a tool commonly used by economists to evaluate the advantages and disadvantages of a particular policy or development decision. Any factors that can't directly be converted to cash value are treated residuals,[13] and are thereby sidelined and removed from the main body of considerations. An implied value for residuals is "deduced" in terms of other benefits foregone or other benefits gained, as perceived by society. Economists have developed a technique known as "contingent evaluation", which is an attempt to evaluate the many non-monetary values of wildlife. An example of contingent valuation would be: "How much would you be willing to pay to prevent the tiger becoming extinct?" (Willingness To Pay or WTP) or: "How much compensation would you need in order to accept the extinction of the tiger?" (Willingness to Accept or WTA).

The WTA value will inevitably be much higher than the WTP value – some may even say that no amount of compensation would be sufficient. (In this case, the value of a species would be infinite, creating some mathematical problems for those analysing the results!) Is it the WTP or the WTA that is "correct"? It is interesting to note that psychologists are not surprised by the difference between WTA and WTP, while some economists do not acknowledge that there is a difference.

Other flaws should be immediately obvious. Does a poor person value the tiger less, simply because he or she cannot pay as much as a rich person? What about the many other species whose fate is linked to that of the tiger?

If consulted at all, society may be asked to make decisions based on incomplete and inadequate information. Our ecological knowledge is by no means complete and we cannot predict the consequences of the loss of a species. It is both unfair and unrealistic to expect the public to place a value on a species, when the consequences of its loss are not understood. The source of the information and the party responsible for carrying out the survey is also important. It is highly unlikely that a questionnaire by an environmental group would ask the same questions and provide the same information as one carried out by a developer. The more information available about a species, the more value people place on it.[14]

Perhaps a more fundamental problem is that contingent valuation

Ecosystems maintain our essential life-support systems

does not ascribe any intrinsic value to species. The developer, polluter, industrialist or commercial exploiter is assumed to have the right to develop, pollute, industrialize and exploit and it is the rest of society who must pay for this not to happen or to be compensated for the results. The fact that compensation is rarely, if ever paid, is a separate issue.

This assumption in favour of the exploiter or polluter denies the rights of future generations to inherit clean air and water, as well as the biodiversity, which the current generation can now enjoy. It seems almost ridiculous that these rights must somehow be "bought back" by the species themselves, yet this is the reasoning underlying the "pay to stay" philosophy which is inherent in economic evaluation.

CONCLUSIONS

Creating commercial value for animals exposes them to market forces, which are completely divorced from biological reality. Market forces have caused the demise of many wild animals, and have restricted the variety of crop species and domestic animals.

Consumers often do not have appropriate information on which to base their choices. Demand can therefore reflect fads and fashions and contain no more overall wisdom than the average consumer. Intensive management, based on economic value and usefulness to humans, is no guarantee of survival, because it does not protect the ecosystems on which wild species depend.

Fortunately, if consumers are well-informed they can choose to boycott products and can help to save species which could otherwise be exploited to extinction.

Protecting the world's remaining natural areas and habitats is not simply a trade-off between development and preservation. Ignoring economic analysis would be unrealistic in today's world, but allowing economic factors to be the main guiding force in conservation policy is dangerous. Wildlands are not "wastelands" simply because they do not generate revenue. They are productive systems, many of which have been used by people for millennia.

The challenge now is how to protect essential ecosystem processes while meeting the needs of a growing population. Many decisions are being made based on economic analysis alone, but economics are just one element in a more complex picture. Protecting free trade and the profits of the developed world, at the expense of the environment, avoids fundamental issues about the distribution of wealth and our responsibilities to future generations, other species and the ecological processes on which we depend.

The developed world has made many grave mistakes in the management of its own wildlife and continues to utilize a disproportionate amount of natural resources. Perhaps those who have profited so much from the destruction of the environment could now be responsible for developing environmentally friendly technologies, and helping to ensure that the same mistakes are not made again.

Notes

1. A. Smith, *Wealth of Nations*, 6th edition.
2. C. W. Clark, *Mathematical Bioresources: The Optimal Management of Renewable*

Resources. New York: Wiley-Interscience, 1990, cited in E. J. Milner-Gulland and R. Mace, *Conservation of Biological Resources*. Oxford: Blackwell Science, 1999.

3. M. H. Glantz, "Man, state and fisheries: an inquiry into some social constraints that affect fisheries management". *Ocean Development and International Law*, vol. 17, pp. 191–270, 1986
4. W. C. Allee (1931). "Animal Aggregations. A study in general sociology". University of Chicago Press, Chicago, 1931, cited in M. Begon, J. L. Harper and C. R. Townsend, *Ecology*. Oxford: Blackwell Science, 1996.
5. Griffiths Norton, "The economics of wildlife conservation policy in Kenya", in E. J. Milner-Gulland and R. Mace, *Conservation of Biological Resources*. Oxford: Blackwell Science, 1999, pp. 279–93.
6. C. W. Clark, "Profit maximization and the extinction of animal species". *Journal of Political Economy*, vol. 81, pp. 950–61, 1973.
7. R. E. Gullison, "Will bigleaf Mahogany be conserved through sustainable use?", 1999, in Milner-Gulland and Mace, *Conservation of Biological Resources*, pp. 193–205.
8. H. Hobbelink, "Biotechnology and the future of World Agriculture". London: Zed Books, 1991, cited in T. M. Swanson and E. B. Barbier, *Economics for the Wilds*. London: Earthscan Publications.
9. Swanson and Barbier, *Economics for the Wilds*, p. 5.
10. Ibid.
11. A. E. Punt and D. S. Butterworth, The effects of future consumption by the Cape fur seal on catches and catch rates of the Cape hakes. 4. Modelling the biological interaction between Cape fur seals *Arcotphalus pusillus pusillus* and the Cape hakes *Merlussius capensis* and *M. paradoxus*. *South African Journal of Marine Science*, vol. 16, pp. 255–75, 1995.
12. R. A. P. Pellew, "The impacts of elephant, giraffe and fire upon the Acacia tortilis woodlands of the Serengeti". *African Journal of Ecology*, vol. 21, pp. 41–74, 1983.
13. J. Adams, *The Emperor's Old Clothes: the curious comeback of cost-benefit analysis*. London: UCL Press, 1992.
14. K. C. Samples, J. A. Dixon and M. M. Gowen, "Information disclosure and endangered species valuation". *Land Economics*, vol. 62, pp. 306–12, 1986, cited in Swanson and Barbier, *Economics for the Wilds*.

3 No Free Lunch

Lindsey Gillson

Increasingly, wildlife conservation has become associated with the "sustainable use" of natural resources. We are told that there is "no free lunch" for wildlife and that it must pay its way. But is this conservation and is it a realistic aim? Can conservation really be replaced by sustainable development? Has the conservationist's expertise been subsumed, leaving the fate of wildlife in the hands of "sustainable developers"? Or is sustainable development merely development as usual, but hidden behind a "green" camouflage? This chapter discusses the concept of sustainable development and compares it with wildlife conservation.

DOES "SUSTAINABLE USE" EQUAL CONSERVATION?

A traditional definition of conservation is:

1. The act or an instance of conserving or keeping from change, loss or injury etc.
2. Protection, preservation, and careful management of natural resources and of the environment.[1]

The emphasis in this definition is on the prevention of damage and loss. There is an underlying acceptance of the intrinsic worth of the environment, because the terms "protection" and "preservation" are not necessarily linked with usefulness to humans. This approach advocates caution in our use of species and the environment. It is a "risk averse" definition, recommending protection rather than exploitation. The problem with this definition is that it fails to acknowledge that natural systems cannot be kept from change. Living things are constantly changing; they are born, reproduce, grow old and die. The birth rate for a species is rarely exactly equal to the death rate, so population sizes will tend to fluctuate. On a geological timescale, climatic changes have profound effects on the distribution and abundance of populations and species.

Conservation may also be defined as:

> The planning and management of resources so as to secure their wise use and continuity of supply, while maintaining and enhancing their quality, value and diversity.[2]

This definition emphasizes the uses which humans can make of natural resources. It assumes that humans can manipulate natural resources in order to increase their usefulness. This definition has much in common with the idea of sustainable development. However, it differs in that any use of natural resources must not decrease quality and diversity.

In 1987, the Brundlant Commission defined Sustainable Development as:

> development which meets the needs of the present without compromising the ability of future generations to meet their own needs.[3]

In other words, each generation should inherit the same as the last. Economists use the concept of capital stock to quantify this inheritance. Capital stock includes both man-made and natural resources, as well as human capital like knowledge and learned skills. Natural resources include fossil fuels and forests, as well as biodiversity, and clean air and water. All of these resources, both man-made and natural can be called aggregate capital stock. The definition of sustainability holds that this stock should not be depleted by current generations.

David Pearce, the economist responsible for the seminal treatise "Blueprint for a Green Economy" and its sequels, defines two types of sustainability: weak and strong.[4] Weak sustainability assumes that resources are interchangeable; as long as the aggregate capital stock remains the same, then we should not worry about its composition. According to this school of thought, it would not matter that biodiversity was lost, as long as it was replaced by an "equivalent" (however that is defined) amount of roads, buildings or any other category of resource.

The strong sustainability argument does not accept that all resources are interchangeable. The ozone layer, which protects humans from the harmful effects of ultra-violet light, and the carbon cycle, which determines how much carbon is present in the atmosphere and consequently influences the rate of global warming, are irreplaceable. Pearce has coined the phrase "critical natural capital" to

Figure 3.1: The sustainability spectrum. Adapted from D. Pearce, (1996) *Blueprint 3: Measuring Sustainable Development*. Earthscan Publications Ltd, London, pp. 18–19.

	TECHNOCENTRIC		**ECOCENTRIC**	
Perspective	Cornucopian: Resource exploitative, growth orientated	Accommodating: Resource conservationist /managerial	Communalist: Resource preservationist	Deep Ecology: Extreme preservationist
Type of economy	Free market	Modified economic growth	Regulated, steady-state economy	Economy heavily-regulated to minimise resource use.
Ethics	Support interest of the individual	Contemporary and future equity a consideration	Interests of the collective are more important than the individual	Nature has intrinsic value.
Management strategies	Main aim is maximum economic growth	Modified economic growth. Measurement of GNP adjusted to include some environmental costs	The aim is zero economic growth and zero population growth	Population reduction and reduce scale of economy.

cover those natural resources which are essential to human well-being, and therefore cannot be substituted by man-made resources.

Pearce expands on his idea of weak and strong sustainability by describing a "sustainability spectrum". At one end of the spectrum, the very weak sustainability end, are those who implicitly trust free market economics. They aim to maximize Gross National Product and assume that all resources are interchangeable. At the other end of the spectrum are those who take an extreme preservationist view. They believe that economies should be heavily regulated to prevent the over-exploitation of natural resources. They also believe that nature has intrinsic value, and does not have to "pay its way".

It is the concept of critical nature capital that is common to conservation and strong sustainability. A lost species cannot be replaced and an entire ecosystem can only be conserved as an intact whole. Pearce says, "loss of biological diversity is perhaps the most important loss of natural capital".

Biodiversity is a measure of the number of species within an ecosystem and their relative abundance. Diversity indices, which are used to compare the diversity of different areas, or changes in diversity over time, compare the number of individuals of each species with the total number of individuals present. A polluted river, for example, tends to have a lower diversity index than a clean one, even if the biomass (weight of living material) remains the same. The polluted river community becomes dominated by pollution tolerant species and biodiversity has been lost.

Biological diversity is not interchangeable with any other type of capital stock. A lost species cannot be replaced with its "equivalent value" in other species. Each species is irreplaceable because it is unique and fulfils a specific role within its community. Natural selection directs an organism's evolution and specializes it for its place in the ecosystem. The biodiversity that we see today is the result of many thousands or millions of years of evolution. It is not possible to convert the "value" of rainforest into financial terms then exchange it for its equivalent in roads, buildings and charcoal. It would be like

SUSTAINABLE DEVELOPMENT POLICY	WILDLIFE CONSERVATION POLICY
Aims to exploit natural resources for human benefit	Aims to conserve and maintain biodiversity, regardless of its utilitarian value.
A spectrum of opinion on exploitation, from implicit faith in free market economics and the aim of economic growth, to controlled markets and a precautionary approach.	Advocates a precautionary approach to resource use. Benefits to humans must not jeopardise essential ecosystem processes, such as geochemical cycles.
A range of opinions, from technocentric to ecocentric	Ecocentric
A spectrum of opinions; at the one extreme, all forms of capital are substitutable. At the other extreme, species are not interchangeable and have intrinsic worth.	Ecocentric Species are not interchangeable.

Figure 3.2: Comparison of sustainable development policy and wildlife conservation policy

trying to use sign language to describe the experience of hearing a symphony.

Concern over biodiversity is common to conservation and some sustainable developers. But within the area of overlap between conservation and sustainable development, there is a fundamental difference in aim. David Pearce says that, "The whole rationale for sustainable development . . . is to raise the standard of living – and especially the standard of living of the least advantaged in society – while at the same time avoiding uncompensated future costs." Conservationists may well agree with these goals, but they are not the sole aim of conservation.

Conservation policies should ultimately benefit both humans and wildlife, but their primary aim is to maintain "biodiversity and ecosystem integrity".[5] Some areas that are of great importance to conservationists are in fact of little interest to developers. They may be too arid to support agriculture and too remote and sparsely populated to be a practical place for the manufacture and marketing of products. Areas like Tsavo National Park in Kenya, have vast potential as conservation areas and can contribute to development by providing jobs in the tourism sector. The area is an important biodiversity centre, because it is here that the northern and southern races of species overlap.[6] The development benefits are a byproduct, not the driving force for the conservation of Tsavo. In contrast, some areas, such as tropical rainforests, are of prime interest to both conservationists and developers, as their biological richness includes species of potential and actual commercial value.

Habitat protection is at the core of the conservationist's remit. Conservationists must decide how large an area of habitat is required to maintain biodiversity and protect ecosystem processes such as geo-chemical cycles. They have to decide whether human activities are threatening these processes and if so, what alternatives are available to local communities. Where habitat and biodiversity conservation impacts on human welfare, conservationists are also concerned with improving the standard of living for local communities. It is here that strong sustainability can inform and aid conservation, by providing ideas about alternative fuels, non-damaging sources of income and improvements to the welfare of local communities.

Far-sighted animal welfare and conservation groups realize that conservation and wildlife protection measures are likely to fail if they are the cause of resentment among those people who live in or at the fringes of protected areas. They can avoid this conflict by helping local communities to develop alternatives. An example would be Care for the Wild International's gift of books to local schools and support of the Ranthambhore Art School, based near Ranthambhore National Park, in Rajasthan, India. Ranthambhore's tigers have become an asset to local artists, who sell their paintings of tigers and other wildlife to the wealthy West.

Conservation can and does improve the standard of living for people – our very lives depend on the ecological processes which conservation aims to safeguard. Conservation, therefore, has certain aims in common with the strong end of the sustainability spectrum; both are concerned with the conservation of biodiversity and the welfare of humans within and around conservation areas. This is reflected in the similarities between the definition of conservation and the definition of sustainable development. But the two terms are not synonymous.

The problem is not the concept of sustainable development per se. It makes perfect sense that conservationists should be involved in and contribute to, the debate about sustainable use. However, it is also essential that they maintain a separate identity, as conservation and wildlife experts. Otherwise, all conservation policies will be diluted and undermined. This is because the sustainability spectrum includes at one extreme those whose ideas are in direct conflict with the aims of conservation; those who believe that man-made capital stock and nature capital are interchangeable. Conservation, with its ecocentric, precautionary approach is in danger of being lost in the whole sustainable development spectrum. By merging wildlife conservation with the sustainability spectrum, the "weak sustainability" camp has the opportunity to pass themselves off as conservationists. The Wise Use Movement is a case in point.

THE WISE USE MOVEMENT: A WOLF IN SHEEP'S CLOTHING

The Wise Use Movement has taken its name from some definitions of conservation similar to that given at the beginning of this chapter ("The planning and management of resources so as to secure their wise use and continuity of supply, while maintaining and enhancing their quality, value and diversity.").[7] However, their ideas are extreme and are diametrically opposed to those of conservationists. The term "wise use" creates the illusion of unity between two irreconcilable philosophies.

The Wise Use Movement sees nature as, at best, a resource to be exploited for the benefit of humans, and at worst as a savage wilderness which needs to be tamed or destroyed for the sake of civilization as we know it. There are various motivations for these extreme views, financial gain being among them. Behavioural ecologist Barbara Maas has researched the extent and effectiveness of the Wise Use Movement. Ranchers, miners, trappers, loggers, fishermen, hunters, whalers, sealers, pro-gun supporters, industry associations and corporate front groups have joined together in the aggressive defensive of free markets.[8]

The Wise Use Movement's seemingly benign message is rapidly gaining acceptance in mainstream culture. Slogans like "Use it or Lose it" and "Wildlife Must Pay to Stay" have been readily accepted by some who feel that they stand to benefit from the exploitation of world's natural resources.

The Wise Use movement focuses its attention on developing countries, as it is here that biodiversity is richest, people are poorest and regulation weakest. The Wise Use ideology encourages "sport" and trophy hunting, as well as the trade in luxury goods like fur and ivory. They use the poverty of indigenous people to justify their actions, while in fact, little effort is made to ensure that profits are made by those who need it most. Members of the Wise Use Movement disguise themselves as conservationists in order to gain respectability and some semblance of responsibility towards wildlife. Their ideology is alien to most true conservationists, but their relentless campaign is causing confusion among the public at large.

ATTITUDES TO NATURAL RESOURCES

The sustainability spectrum is a representation of the range of attitudes towards natural resources. It reflects human opinions, not the actual state of natural resources; there is simply no room within its framework to incorporate such information. As our understanding of ecosystems improves, it might be expected that this range of views would converge. However, this does not appear to be occurring and in fact the debate over sustainable use is becoming increasingly polarized.

In order to understand why this is happening, it is helpful to look at the ideas underlying the sustainability spectrum. There is also a whole spectrum of attitudes towards the exploitation of natural resources.

John Adams describes four "myths of nature":[9]

1. Nature is benign and robust. It will return to its "equilibrium" level after exploitation or any other perturbation. This view is exploitative and is the one held by the venture capitalists, who are in the "extreme weak" end of the sustainability spectrum.
2. Nature is capricious and that the results of an action are something of a lottery. According to this view, it is pointless trying to predict the consequences of a given level of harvesting, so we should simply take what we want.
3. Nature has critical loads, or thresholds; it is robust up to those limits, but once they are exceeded, the resource will be destroyed.
4. Nature is precarious and can easily be destroyed. A precautionary approach to exploitation should be taken, involving predicting what would happen under a worst case scenario. This view is at the extremely strong end of the sustainability spectrum.

SUSTAINABLE USE – THEORY AND PRACTICE

Renewable natural resources are those which can grow and replace themselves. Examples are fisheries and forests. The theory of sustainable use is that the rate of harvesting should not be greater than the rate of replenishment. The Maximum Sustainable Yield (MSY) is the maximum amount which can be harvested without depletion of the population. Predicting the MSY has been a major challenge to population biologists, who have attempted to model populations and their responses to different levels of harvesting. Their aim is to predict the largest yield which can be taken from a population without endangering the resource.

In order to do this, it is necessary to try and understand how populations grow and change. In population modelling, it is assumed that populations grow logistically; this means that they grow exponentially until the population reaches half of the carrying capacity of the habitat, then the rate of growth slows. At the carrying capacity, the rate of growth of the population is zero.

For several reasons, attempting to harvest at the Maximum Sustainable Yield is dangerous. First, the population models are only as good as the data that is input. In many cases, it is not possible to accurately count the population size of the species to be harvested. It is highly unlikely that the behaviour and reproductive biology of exploited species will be understood in sufficient detail that the effects of harvesting can be predicted. So the starting point of the whole model must have a very wide margin of error.

Secondly, the harvested population will also be affected by other species higher and lower in the food chain, and the same limitations in knowledge of population size, behaviour and reproductive biology will apply to them.

Thirdly, we must ask whether we accurately understand the diet of the species to be harvested and its predators. For fish species, preyed on by seals, for example, how much trouble and expense will be spent in accurately understanding the seal's diet, its preferred food species?

Fourthly, some of the factors which determine population size, such as outbreaks of disease or severe weather conditions, or drought, cannot be foreseen. Quotas must be set in advance, so that the necessary number of employees to harvest this quota can be hired, and the required capacity for processing, treatment, distribution and sale of the harvest can be developed. Quotas must, by necessity, be set in advance. They are therefore not responsive to unforeseen events.

The result is that the confidence limits of MSY are huge. An apparently "sustainable" level of harvesting can cause the depletion of a species.

Even if a "safe" quota could be predicted, in practice such quotas

Figure 3.3: Population growth rate and the theory of maximum sustainable yield

Population growth is highest when population size is half the carrying capacity. Harvesting rate H_2 is higher than the population growth rate and depletes the population. Harvesting rate H_1 leads to an equilibrium population at N_{MSY}, the population size at which the rate of growth is maximum. Harvesting at H_1 gives the maximum sustainable yield.

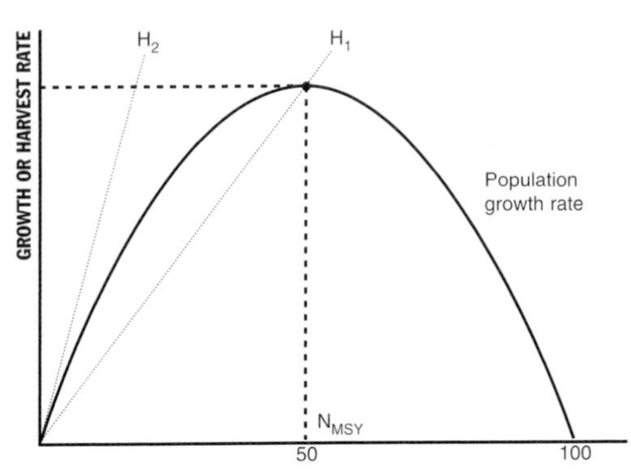

are often exceeded. Commercial harvesters, processors and distributors need to exceed a minimum throughput if they are to remain economically viable. Restricting supply drives prices up and fuels poaching and illegal trade. Enforcement is practically impossible, and smugglers are ingenious. As populations become depleted, prices increase even more, because the species attains a "scarcity value". Small animal populations are much more vulnerable to extinction; they can suffer from inbreeding depression, which means that genetic variability is lost. The social structure may be disrupted and reproduction may suffer.

There are various attitudes to this huge margin of error in the prediction of a sustainable yield. If enough data were available, in theory, it would be possible to postulate a "worst case scenario" in which all of the known factors were stacked against the harvested population. This precautionary approach would advocate a much lower off-take and a flexible, responsive approach to quota setting. The difficulties of applying this in practice would be that by the time the data had been collected and the predictions made, they would already be out of date; quotas for this year must inevitably be calculated using previous years data. The expense of collecting sufficient data may prove prohibitive and there are problems in enforcing low quotas.

In practice, therefore, the rate of harvesting is influenced by many factors, including the price of the resource being harvested, the demand for it, the size of the industry to be supported by the resource and the availability of alternatives. None of these factors are related to the resilience of the population being harvested and its ability to withstand exploitation.

Once the consumptive use of wildlife becomes commercialized, and international trade is involved, there is little to prevent over-exploitation. Commercial use is driven by market forces, which have no connection to the rate of regeneration of animal populations. The

If the harvesting rate increases from H_1 to H_2, for example because of illegal harvesting, the harvested population will become depleted. If population size is P_2 instead of P_1, for example because population size has been over-estimated, or a catastophic event has reduced the population, then harvesting at H_1 will deplete the population.

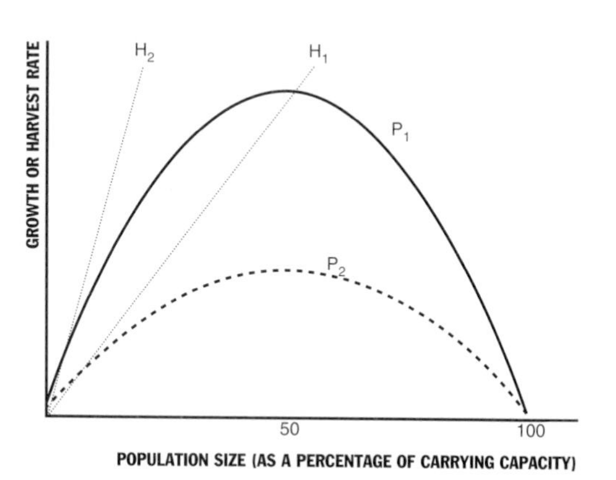

Figure 3.4: The effects of uncertainty on predicting the maximum sustainable yield

reproductive rate of animals and plants has intrinsic limits which cannot be exceeded.

Commercial, consumptive use of wildlife is rarely if ever sustainable, particularly when international trade is involved. The "Sustainable Users" arguments simply do not comply with biological reality. Devastated populations of whales, tigers, elephants (pre-ivory ban), rhinos and many fish-stocks are a testament to the failure of "sustainable" use.

WHO "OWNS" WILDLIFE?

One of the problems of harvesting natural resources is the question of ownership. Who owns wildlife and who should be allowed to sell it?

Some natural resources, such as the atmosphere, the ocean beyond the continental shelf and some grazing lands do not "belong" to anybody and are known as the global commons. These open access resources are extremely vulnerable to over-exploitation. Garrett Hardin summed up the problem in terms of "The Tragedy of the Commons". He uses the example of an area of common grazing land to explain why open access resources tend to become degraded. Each commoner would gain if they agreed to limit the number of cows or sheep which they kept on the common, thus ensuring that the land was not over-grazed and degraded. However, if no rules are in place, or if there are no means of enforcing them, then it is to each commoner's immediate benefit to keep as many animals as they can on the common. Those who limit the number of animals for the sake of the resource achieve nothing, because the degradation continues regardless of their self-sacrifice.

Hardin's idea has received some criticism for failing to distinguish between communally owned and open access resources; in the former case, communal ownership and responsibility can serve to protect and sustain a resource. In the latter, no one is responsible and the use of the resource becomes a free for all. Most "commons" are not open-access: only certain members of the local population have commoners' rights and can graze their animals on common land. There generally tends to be a more responsible attitude towards communally owned areas than open-access ones. However, Hardin's idea has been borne out in the case of the high seas, which are open access outside of the 200-mile coastal zones. On the one hand, they have been used as a dumping ground for nuclear waste, sewage and other refuse, because no rules were in place to prevent this. On the other hand, many fish stocks are collapsing because of over-exploitation.

It could be argued that allotting ownership of natural resources therefore would encourage a more sustainable approach. But this too, has many difficulties. Who should own natural resources? And if alternative investments offer better returns, what would prevent an owner from selling off or destroying the resource and investing these one-off profits elsewhere?

There are two main issues at stake. The first is the question of property rights. Most patents for biological resources are held by the developed countries, despite the fact that the vast majority of biodiversity is present in the tropics. But as yet there is no legal mechanism in place to prevent foreign corporations from profiting from the rich biodiversity of poor tropical countries.

Even if this difficulty could be resolved, however, there would still be no guarantee that the resource would be preserved. As discussed above, there are difficulties in predicting a safe level of harvesting. In addition, the owner of the resource may decide that it is optimal to cash-in the entire value of the resource and invest the income elsewhere. Economists use the discount rate to predict how much a resource will be worth in the future. If the discount rate is high, then resources rapidly decline in value over time. In this case, it will be more profitable for the resource owner to harvest it to extinction, then invest the revenue elsewhere. Slow growing species, such as large mammals and hardwood trees, are especially vulnerable to this type of over-exploitation. This mechanism explains the replacement of broad-leaved woodland with faster growing soft-wood species in Britain.

Fortunately, the slowest growing species are often the largest and most spectacular. They can generate revenue from non-lethal means such as tourism. Tourism can provide income from wildlife without killing it, though it must be developed and managed carefully to minimize negative impact on wildlife and habitat. Also, if local people are to benefit, it is essential that tourist operations do not become concentrated in the hands of large (mainly foreign) tour operators.

CONCLUSION

The concept of Biodiversity has become an increasingly important element of conservation philosophy. It is the conservationist's acknowledgement that "natural resource capital" is not exchangeable. Therefore on the "sustainability spectrum", described by Pearce, conservationists will by definition fall into the most extreme category, because they will not accept that species are exchangeable. Therefore, in the sustainability debate, conservationists will always be classed as extremists, whose aims are likely to be marginalized. It is therefore essential that conservation maintains a separate identity to sustainable development.

There is growing pressure for wildlife to "pay to stay". But harvesting wildlife can threaten its very existence. It is difficult to set a safe level of harvesting, because population biology cannot accurately determine population sizes and predict the result of particular levels of harvesting. There are also problems of enforcing quotas. A restriction in the supply of a product can increase its value, creating an incentive for illegal harvesting. In practice, sustainable use may not be realistic.

Habitat destruction and degradation, pollution, international trade and a growing human population are all threatening the world's wildlife. Commercial, lethal exploitation, whether apparently "sustainable" or not, can only increase the risk of biodiversity loss. A strong conservation policy is essential to protecting the critical nature capital on which human welfare depends. Humans will not benefit in the long term if nature is degraded in the name of "sustainable" use.

Notes

1. *Collins English Dictionary*, 8th edn. Oxford: William Collins & Co. Ltd.
2. M. Allaby, *Dictionary of the Environment*, 2nd edn. New York: New York University Press, 1983, p. 123.
3. World Commission on Environment and Development (WCED), *Our Common Future*. Geneva: Oxford University Press, 1987, p. 43.
4. D. Pearce, *Blueprint 3: Measuring Sustainable Development*. London: Earthscan Publications, 1986, p. 18.
5. J. Robinson, G. Francis, R. Legge and S. Lerner, Defining a sustainable society: Values, principles and definitions. Working paper no. 1. Sustainable Society Project, Waterloo, Canada: University of Waterloo, 1990.
6. D. Sheldrick, personal communication, 1998.
7. M. Allaby, *Dictionary of the Environment*, 2nd edn. New York: New York University Press, 1983, p. 123.
8. B. Maas, *What is the Wise Use Movement and how does it affect animals globally?* International Fund for Animal Welfare, 1996.
9. J. Adams, *Risk*. London: UCL Press, 1995.
10. G. Hardin,"The tragedy of the commons". *Science*, vol. 162, pp. 1243–8, 1968.

4 Captive Breeding

Samantha Scott

The stated aim of captive breeding is to maintain an ex situ population of endangered species until such time that they can be released back into their natural habit. This chapter examines whether or not this is a realistic aim. It examines how captive breeding programmes work, the numbers of animals breeding and those species which have a poor track record breeding. This chapter also discusses the other difficulties these programmes face in practice and whether the benefit for species and the individuals offset the disadvantages. Solutions and alternatives to the current practices are also discussed.

In keeping with their stated *raison d'être*, zoological institutions and wildlife parks are increasingly promoting themselves as centres for the breeding of endangered species.

The main declared aim of captive breeding is to maintain an ex situ population of an endangered species until such time that the habitat (or something approximating to the habitat) can sustain the species once again.

The purpose of this chapter is to examine the realities of captive breeding programmes and ask the questions:

- How are captive breeding programmes organized and structured?
- How widespread are these programmes?
- How many species are being successfully bred?
- What are the difficulties experienced by these programmes?
- What are the pitfalls for the species and for the individuals?
- How realistic are the aims of captive breeding?
- How do in situ measures and ex situ captive breeding compare?

Other chapters will deal with the message of zoos and wildlife parks, whether they are achieving all they claim to be achieving and the dangers and drawbacks of the re-introduction of captive bred animals.

Captive breeding programmes only constitute a small part of a zoo's structure, although the impression given is that they are far more significant. This chapter aims to put captive breeding into perspective so that when we are faced with the good news of the birth of another endangered animal we can be aware of its significance, how it has come about and whether or not we are justified in celebrating.

STRUCTURE AND ORGANIZATION OF CAPTIVE BREEDING PROGRAMMES

The objective of the International Union for the Conservation of Nature and Natural Resources (IUCN) is to promote and encourage the protection and sustainable use of living resources. The Species Survival Commission (SSC) is part of the IUCN and a subgroup of the SSC is the Captive Breeding Specialist Group (CBSG). The role of the CBSG is to preserve from extinction those species identified as endangered by the IUCN. To this end the CBSG attempts to identify problem areas, co-ordinate global efforts and analyse population viability.

Individual countries and continents have their own conservation committees: The American Zoo and Aquarium Association (AZAA) have a standing committee which oversees the AZAA Species Survival Plans (SSPs) which are the foundation of their conservation programme. The SSPs are plans for individual species which address demographic and genetic problems associated with maintaining small populations for long periods of time.

In Europe, the Europaisches Erhaltungszucht Program (EEP) is the SSP equivalent and the Australian Species Management Program (APMP), its Australian counterpart.

Amongst such a forest of acronyms it is hardly surprising if communications are not always maintained between the various groups despite best efforts and intentions. One author states rather gently:

> It is not always easy to detect the relationship among the various groups.[1]

The keeping of studbooks provides animal records – matings, births, deaths and survivals. For a given species survival plan (of any acronym) the studbook keeper is a named individual with responsibility to provide accurate information, maintain close contact with all participating institutions and ensure that information is recorded properly and on time. In some cases, the studbook keeper is the same person as the species co-ordinator for a given species.

The studbook records are used to formulate a "master plan" for a species based on genetic and demographic analysis of those records, i.e. plans for breeding and transfer.

But much captive breeding goes on without the master plans and species survival programmes. Some of it involves endangered animals who are not involved in any co-ordinated programme or for which a co-ordinated plan has not yet been drawn up. Some captive breeding involves species which are neither considered to be endangered nor vulnerable.

The reasons for this breeding may include:

1. Accidental mating
2. Whim of collection owner simply because they like that given species.
3. A "no contraceptive–no control" policy on reproduction
4. "Production" of baby animals to increase turnstile numbers and visitor appeal.

CAN THIS KIND OF CAPTIVE BREEDING BE REGARDED AS RESPONSIBLE?

- It is a drain on the resources of the zoological institution.
- Accidental mating may produce offspring which are inbred and therefore useless or detrimental to the genetic integrity of a population.
- Whims of owners simply result in overcrowding and depletion of resources. "Baby" animals are all very appealing and may be useful for public relations exercises but there is a high infant mortality rate amongst many captive bred neonates which brings into question their welfare and management and possible subsequent distress or disturbance to the parent carer.
- Many "babies" are, in reality, surplus to requirements and may have to be euthanased or moved on.[2]

HOW MANY SPECIES ARE INVOLVED IN CAPTIVE BREEDING PROGRAMMES?

Data on the breeding of captive species is passed on to other zoos and organizations in a less than uniform way. The International Zoo Yearbook,[3] from which most of this section's data is taken, attempts to provide lists of wild animals bred in captivity (the 1998 yearbook chronicles 1994 and part of 1995) and "multiple generation captive births". However, their task is made difficult by the fact that:

> Only about half of all collections reporting their breeding results provided any record of multiple generation births . . .[3]

And, of course, many collections will not report at all. There is no record of how many zoos report to the International Zoo Yearbook. Some data is collected via questionnaire, but is largely dependant upon the way records are kept at individual institutions. The owners of the so-called roadside zoos in Ontario, Canada, for example often did not even know how many animals they had in their collections, let alone record numbers.[4] In terms of trying to assess survival of species born in captivity the problem is compounded by the fact that:

> Not all institutions indicate whether or not their animals survive . . .[3]

Some apparently only record the young which have been reared successfully,[3] which will bias any analysis in favourable light towards the institution and towards captive breeding generally. Further difficulties arise because:

> zoos differ in their methods of record.[3]

None of this is perhaps surprising, but it does highlight the fact that much of the information the public receives about breeding in zoos and wildlife parks may not necessarily be very accurate.

Because the endangered/vulnerable species for which there are species survival plans (or equivalent) have a single studbook recording world-wide (participating) zoo information, these should be more accurate, but for how many species does such an arrangement exist?

According to the Yearbook, between 1994 and 1995, 142 species are listed in international studbooks. Of these, 25 are bird species, one amphibian, one invertebrate species and five reptiles; the remainder being mammals. In 1996 (the last year for which figures are available there were 28 bird species and 107 mammals.

As David Hancocks pointed out in Adieu to the Zoo?[5] this creates a distortion in the minds of the public as to the true composition of life on this planet, and, worse, the numbers of those species which are threatened. For instance, amphibians are represented by 20,000 species in the wild and frog species are declining dramatically worldwide, yet there are only eight species in zoos and only one of these (Puerto Rican Crested Toad) has a Species Survival Plan.

The Captive Breeding Specialist Group estimates that 3000–5000 non-fish vertebrates are at significant risk of extinction over the next two to five generations;[6] 10,000 to 12,000 zoos and wildlife parks world-wide carry, between them all, in the order of 150 international studbooks (regional studbooks do exist).

This is not to detract from the work already done or to deny that anyone in the field does not have a concept of the overwhelming task facing conservationists in trying to halt the decline in biodiversity. Nor does it refute the claim of "well, we have to start somewhere" and that "150 studbooks are better than none". But it does put into perspective how much of those 10,000–12,000 institutions are actively contributing to the task and how many species are being kept in captivity which are serving no conservation purpose at all.

The figures also back up claims that zoos are spending large amounts of money and expertise on breeding those species which continue to "draw" the public, i.e. the megafauna, those which have cute and saleable offspring, and those which are perceived as glamorous. To quote Hancocks again:

animals that are in any case more important to zoos than to nature.[5]

In a final word on record-keeping: 60 of those 142 international studbooks listed in the Yearbook appeared to have no up-to-date data or stated that data was being collected; several were without a studbook keeper at all.

HOW MANY SPECIES ARE BEING SUCCESSFULLY BRED?

Studbook data aside, the International Zoo Yearbook also carries the previously described list of animals born in captivity and those multiple generation births which the zoos may or may not have recorded.

Of all the species listed as having been bred in zoos and parks world-wide, only 308 species which had bred were on the IUCN lists; these are not all critically endangered – the lists include lower risk categories including a data deficient category.

Of all the species which had been recorded as breeding during 1994–5 there were approximately 550 occasions on which an institution failed to keep any offspring of a given species alive. Species which appeared, on the strength of the data available, to fare particularly badly included the Arctic fox, ruffed lemur, the golden lion tamarin, the Bornean orangutan and various species of wolves. The small cats such as the serval, the lynx and the bobcat had offspring which frequently failed to survive. Out of 41 hippo born in captivity, 14 failed to survive; out of 16 black bear born only four survived. Seven Asian elephants were born during this time period (1994–5) and one died, but only four African elephants were born and one of these died. Out of 22 polar bear born in captivity, 16 died.

So, although there are undoubtedly a large number of certain species being bred one must examine the outcome of the breeding and ask the questions:

- Do the offspring survive?
- For how long do they survive on average (quoted survival rates will increase if one alters whether survival means for the first week or the first year of life)?
- Out of the total number of this species being kept in captivity, how many are bred and how many offspring survive? (There are approximately 600 Polar bears in captivity – only 22 offspring were produced.)
- Are the populations self-sustaining? If not, animals have to be imported from the wild.
- What is going wrong with breeding in these institutions if large numbers of offspring are failing to survive and some species are failing to breed?
- What are the difficulties with these programmes?

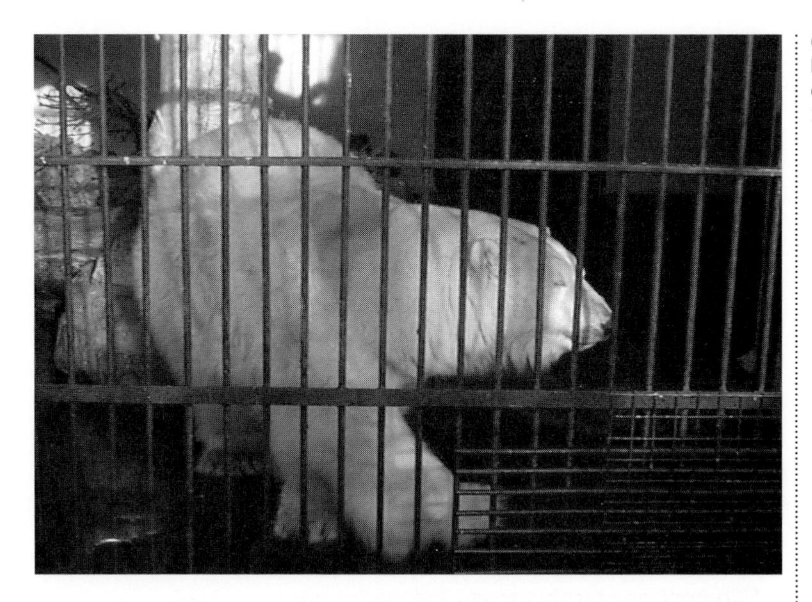

Out of 22 polar bears born in captivity during 1994–5, 16 died

One of the difficulties already discussed is the keeping, transfer and communication of accurate information.

Another is that animals need to be transferred, usually large distances, in order to be on "breeding loan" at another participating zoo. This creates transport stress for the animal; additionally there are risks in tranquillising species for capture and movement. The animal must then adapt to new surroundings, new attendants, very probably a new climate and possibly new conspecifics (one certainly – the intended mate!). All of this, not to be too flippant about it, would be likely to dampen the ardour of the most libidinous individual. However, some species will breed consistently well in captivity, e.g. African lions, and many species will breed under difficult conditions. Far from using breeding as a reflection of welfare, it should be remembered that the need to reproduce is a powerful driving force which shapes much of the behaviour and many of the adaptations of animal species. It should also be remembered that humans can and do reproduce under the most appalling conditions of war, famine, disease and deprivation.

So, ability to breed in captivity should not be taken as a measure of welfare. It simply reflects whether or not:

1. The species is suited to breeding in captivity per se
2. The environment, management, timing is appropriate
3. Fertility is compromized by disease, inappropriate nutrition, etc.

In addition to these problems, there is the issue of keeping offspring alive once born. Sometimes, zoos resort to hand rearing, which can cause its own difficulties and reduce prospects for survival and re-introduction to the group. Consequent to hand rearing, over familiarization with man can be dangerous from the attendant point of view and dangerous from the disease transmission perspective (zoonosis and reverse zoonosis). Inappropriate management of the parents once the offspring are born may give rise to either the dam or the sire killing the young. Disturbance of the dam, inappropriate handling/management, too much public attention or inexperience of the dam with no conspecific support (e.g. allo mothering in elephants) may cause the dam to abandon, mis-mother or inadvertently injure the youngster.

To exemplify some of the difficulties with breeding in captivity let us look at the elephant. The elephant is a common "flagship" species in many zoos. Fortunately, some zoos now accept that it is not appropriate to keep single or even two or three elephants in a zoo and that managing elephants in family groups is a more sensible approach which may increase the well being of captive individuals. Despite the high number of elephants in zoos world-wide, we have seen that numbers of calves born is very low.

The reasons for this are as follows:

1. Bull elephants are difficult and dangerous to keep in captivity. Bull Asian elephants show a regular physiological and behavioural phenomenon called musth. During this time the bull often becomes reluctant to eat, vocalizes, and, amongst other signs, may become very aggressive. This is not a breeding time and elephants in musth should not be mixed with cows and contact with people is likely to result in injury or death. Musth occurs at the same time of year for an individual bull and begins from 10–15 years of age. In captive elephants these periods may be prolonged and usually last from 6–12 weeks but have been known for up to year.[7] African elephants also show periods of increased aggression, but this is not as distinct as musth, although arguably just as dangerous.
2. Natural mating by leaving bull and cow together can result in injury to the cow if she will not co-operate. This often means that, in practice, mating has to be artificially manipulated by judging the cow's readiness to mate. This is not as reliable as natural mating.
3. Libido problems are common in captive cow elephants.[7]
4. Similarly, bull elephants are frequently uninterested in mating, especially if subject to harsh training techniques or punishment or chaining.
5. Infertility due to reproductive tract disease.

Failure for calves to survive may be due to:

1. First time breeders often have difficulty giving birth. In the wild

they would retire with several "allo mothers" who act in a kind of "aunt" capacity; this is not always possible to include in a birth process in the zoo.
2. There is a high incidence of dystocia (difficult birth) in zoo elephants.[7]
3. Some first time breeders (in common with other species) may react in alarm towards their calf and attack it.

WHAT ARE THE PITFALLS OF CAPTIVE BREEDING, FOR THE SPECIES AND FOR THE INDIVIDUAL?

Although we have seen that the outcome of much captive breeding is simply to produce more animals (for whatever purpose) the aim of modern captive breeding programmes should obviously be much more than this. Where captive breeding is not co-ordinated, managed and run by people who have a knowledge of the principles of genetics and genetic variability, the risks to the future of species involved are obvious. Inbreeding is one, oft quoted, outcome of poor breeding programmes and a term much coined by pet owners to account for behavioural and physical problems with their cats and dogs. Inbreeding decreases genetic variability and sooner or later tends to result in a population which carries one or more traits which equip it poorly for survival. These may be reproductive, behavioural or physical traits. It should be remembered that natural selection of a mate does not occur in a captive situation; the choice of mate.

Small numbers of animals making up the "founder population" (i.e. those from which it is possible to breed) limit the size of the gene pool and this is one of the difficulties faced by institutions trying to breed a self sustaining population from a few animals. Another possible pitfall of a controlled breeding programme may result from the aim to keep genes from each animal so that they will not be lost through "genetic drift". This aim is all well and good, but in practice this means encouraging poorly breeding animals to breed. If those animals are not breeding well because of some trait which means that poor fertility will be passed on, then the production of partly fertile or infertile animals may be all that is achieved. These may continue to survive and have their breeding manipulated whilst in a captive environment, but they will not constitute a healthy, fecund population for release into the wild.

The maintenance of behavioural integrity is also threatened in the captive situation. Many zoos do not simulate natural cycles of light or feeding patterns to encourage development and continuation of natural behaviours. Socially complex and long lived species (e.g. primates and elephants) which have an extended learning curve (based on the size of the brain at birth relative to its mature size, for example, the elephant's brain is 35% of the mature adult size at birth, indicating a high degree of early learning) are unlikely to be exposed

Many zoo and circus animals develop behavioural problems, linked to a lack of stimulation within the captive environment

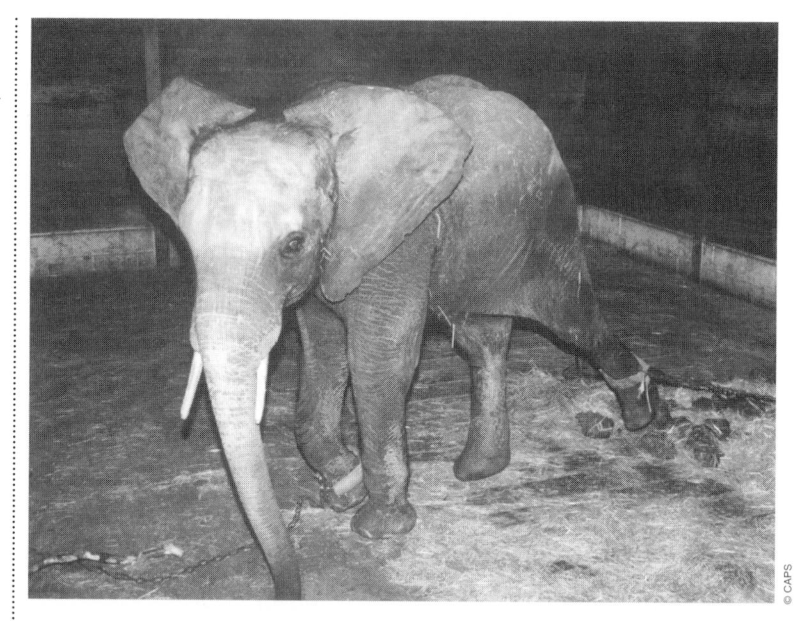

© CAPS

to a steep early learning curve in a zoo setting. The concern is that, even if animals are raised by their natural mothers, because the range of behaviours which can be performed are limited, fewer and fewer behaviours are passed on from generation to generation. If animals are hand reared, maintenance of behavioural integrity is more profoundly threatened. In other words, successive generations of captive bred animals behave less and less like their wild counterparts. They are not tamed, they are not domesticated; they are in a sort of behavioural limbo.

Relying on small captive populations is a dangerous gamble; the parentage of wild caught founder animals is not known so programmes may be starting with related animals (genetic fingerprinting may be one way over this hurdle). We have already seen how animals transported large distances may be at risk or may not co-operate with the programme's choice of mate.

Another pitfall for the species as a whole is the issue of wild capture. In the past, obviously, all animals were wild caught and formed the basis of today's captive populations. However, some of these populations are not self-sustaining for the reasons stated and some animals still have to be imported from the wild. According to the data supplied to the *International Zoo Yearbook* by studbook keepers (those 82 out of 142 who supplied up-to-date information), 24 species were imported from the wild between 1994 and 1995. These include the golden headed lion tamarin, the aye-aye, gorilla, cheetah, sand cat, leopard, polar bear, maned wolf, and the black and the white rhino. Although it is mainly single animals which are reported to have been imported, one has to consider the realities of wild capture. Although it is possible, it is highly improbable that only one individual was sought, captured and transported. The expense of capture, transport, quarantine and paperwork means that settling for one animal which may not survive, darting, sedating and moving is unlikely.

When we are considering very small populations of endangered species this loss to the wild species may be critical. Can zoos justify that the importation of animals into their programmes gives the species a better chance of survival than leaving that animal in the wild? Can they prove that it is so? That animal may have been a critical individual in the local population/group and its removal may have had all sorts of consequences in the long and short term not only for the species but for the local habitat as a knock-on effect. Article 9 of the Biodiversity Convention suggests that removal of populations from the wild for captive breeding should only be undertaken as a last resort, when it can be clearly demonstrated that in situ measures will not work on their own.

TO WHOM DO THE ZOOLOGICAL COMMUNITY DEMONSTRATE THIS JUSTIFICATION?

Already touched upon above, but of paramount importance when considering what captive breeding is achieving for each species, is the change in the species as it progresses through successive generations in a captive bred environment. Those individuals which survive and breed in captivity may be those best adapted to captivity. Survival is not due to "survival of the fittest", but due to medical intervention and prophylaxis. What consequences will there be for re-introduction of that species? Will it even be the same species? How much can man tamper with the genetics of a species and still be left with animals which can be released into the wild? Disease contracted in captivity could become endemic in the captive population and be symptomless after some years, yet still remain dangerous to a wild susceptible population as in the case of the golden lion tamarin described in the chapter on re-introduction. The pitfalls and dangers of re-introduction described in that chapter are already proving to be pertinent in the attempted release of certain species into the wild.

For an individual animal the price to pay for captive breeding may be just as high. As a wild caught animal, the individual will experience the distress of capture, separation from the group, transport, confinement, unfamiliar food, noises, smells and sights. Adaptation to captivity, introduction to a new group, to the presence of attendants and the public must impose the kind of environmental and behavioural stress on these animals that we could only begin to imagine. We can see the results of such stressors in many of the zoo exhibits holding animals displaying disturbed behaviours such as stereotypes, self mutilations, regurgitation, aggression and depression (withdrawal). These individuals may not even be first generation wild caught animals, but those bred in, and purported to be "used to", captivity. The effects of captivity on wild caught animals may be reasonably assumed to be more profound. Although it would appear to be common sense to assume that wild animals will suffer when kept in confinement, many zoological institutions will still insist that this is not the case. This is in spite of the fact that they are unable to express most of their natural range of behaviours and are subjected to the kind of limbo which means that they can neither escape nor attack that which causes them fear or frustration (man or other adjacent species). Or at least, it is not the case until it is proven. These assumptions, we are told, are anthropomorphic. Well, no one human can ever describe how another human would feel being in prison, but nobody has ever had to "prove" that it is a significant punishment and source of distress. We assume so because we feel that we would not like it and, because we have the same physiology, stress responses and behavioural repertoire, we accept this assumption. The physiology and stress responses of animals are sufficiently close to ours to allow them to be used in laboratories all over the world to test drugs and produce animal models of disease which are then extrapolated to the human situation. So why should other assumptions about animals be so far off the mark? Assumptions are what science is based upon. Except when it suits scientists to say otherwise. The problem of surplus animals in captive breeding is an increasing one: "Captive breeding has resulted in the zoo issue of the 90s".[2]

Zoos are simply not equipped to look after the large numbers of easily bred animals. The surplus animals may fall into the hands of unscrupulous dealers and end up in private collections, unlicensed "zoos", circuses or in the canned hunting industry where they would be shot by hunters for trophies. Recently, a private trader was quoted as saying that the current US trade in exotics is worth $150 million a year; not all of this is from zoos, but a large number of animals are purportedly on offer for sport and the pet trade. Circuses themselves engage in breeding their captive species and surplus circus animals have been found in private collections or even in someone's backyard. Euthanasia is the only other option, unless constructive contraception and management is utilized to reduce the problem.

WHY DO SURPLUSES OCCUR?

Sometimes there is genuine error, sometimes mismanagement or poor judgement and sometimes breeding is deliberately encouraged to produce cute offspring to draw the public into the zoo. The problem occurs when the youngster is no longer so cute and is competing for space with the other adults, who may not, in any case, tolerate the presence of young (e.g. ursids).

HOW REALISTIC ARE THE AIMS OF CAPTIVE BREEDING?

We have already seen that there are inherent problems with the principles of trying to retain genetic variability; one may maintain the gene pool and 90% of the genetic variation of the founder population, but will that population be viable in the wild?

If the aim were simply to maintain a circulating captive population then for many species that is probably realistic, but that is not what is claimed by zoological institutions.

Re-introduction of captive bred and maintained species is the stated ultimate goal of captive breeding programmes. I have already touched upon the issues which make re-introduction questionable; endemic disease, fundamental changes in the traits of the captive animals and their ability to adapt to the wild. A recent paper discussing the problems of surpluses created by captive breeding stated that re-introduction was not a viable option. In fact it has been a viable option, but only for a handful of species, and the science of re-introduction is still in the experimental stages. Therefore we have to venture that the aims of captive breeding are not based so much on realism as on a desperate hope that things will turn out well in the end. We all hope so.

HOW DO IN SITU MEASURES COMPARE WITH EX SITU CAPTIVE BREEDING?

Article 9 of the Biodiversity Convention states that *ex situ* measures for conservation, including those carried out in zoos, are "predominantly for the purpose of complementing in situ measures". The country of origin is stated to be the preferred site for such measures.

This should be obvious from many viewpoints:

1. Animals are not removed from the population as a whole.
2. The effect of animal upon habitat and vice versa can be clearly studied.
3. The possible reasons for the decline of the species/habitat can be discovered, witnessed and researched.
4. Measures to halt the decline can be tackled and results judged much more quickly than by re-introduction alone.
5. Animals can usually be maintained in a wild, natural habitat. Although the degree of management and interference varies from programme to programme, the animals are at least surrounded by their native flora and fauna, do not have to adapt to a different climate, are not subject to the attentions of the public and other alien stimuli and are usually maintained in an extensive setting whereby they can exercise most of their natural behaviours.
6. Apart from the risk of reverse zoonosis if man should come too

close to some species, "new diseases" are unlikely to be introduced.

Ex situ measures may become necessary when:

1. War or natural disaster impede in situ measures, putting at risk the lives of workers and decimating populations and habitats beyond the scope of foreseeable regeneration.
2. In situ methods fail to halt the decline of a given species because of environmental change.
3. Political and cultural obstacles prevent progress being made *in situ*.

However, it must be remembered, that unless such difficulties can be overcome at some time in the future or unless there is a prospect of the habitat regenerating or a new one being found, captive breeding in zoos is a waste of resources.

SOLUTIONS?

The danger of the present situation is that zoos and wildlife parks are using vast resources on breeding small numbers of species and that these resources may have been directed away from in situ measures which tackle the heart of the problem. Despite their protestations to the contrary, zoos are still menageries. The only difference is that their Public Relations are more efficient and some of them do a little serious captive breeding and research on the side. Whilst the turnstile takings determine their choice of exhibit, zoos say that they have no choice but to maintain the variety and the megafauna in their collections. Imaginative use of multimedia techniques, virtual reality jungles and oceans, interactive games and wildlife footage is likely to draw far greater crowds and achieve higher standards of education and understanding. Teach the public that theirs is not the right to see animals in captivity, but there are a few species which are being bred in captivity because there is no other choice. Show them the close-circuit/infra red footage of these animals in extensive, natural surroundings. The zoo becomes the "theme park" with a serious conservation message and all its research and scientific staff operate at the breeding centre. The park funds the breeding centre and the breeding centre works closely with the in situ team. Pie in the sky? No more than supposing that slothful, maladjusted animals are going to one day repopulate this decimated Planet Earth and recreate all that has been lost.

Notes

1. William J. Boever, "Medical input into species survival plans". In *Zoo and Wild Animal Medicine*, Current Therapy, p. 11, ed. M. E. Fowler. Saunders, 1978.
2. A. R. Glatson, The control of zoo populations with specific reference to primates. *Animal Welfare*, vol. 7, pp. 269–81, 1998.
3. *The International Zoo Yearbook*, Royal Zoological Society, Regent's Park, 1998.
4. S. Lindley, While Rome burns . . . A report into conditions of the zoos of Ontario. Zoocheck Canada, WSPA Canada, 1997.
5. D. Hancocks, *Adieu to the Zoo?* Proceedings of Conservation and Animal Welfare – A New Era in Europe? London School of Economics, 1995.
6. U. S. Seal, "Increasing risks pose increasing challenges", *CBSG News*, vol. 2(3), p. 1, 1991.
7. Michael J. Schmidt, "Breeding elephants in captivity". In Zoo and Wild Animal Medicine, *Current Therapy*, pp. 445–8, ed. M. E. Fowler. Saunders, 1978.

5 Re-introduction of Captive Bred Animals to the Wild: is the Modern Ark Afloat?

Rob Laidlaw

Most species which zoos breed are not endangered. Return to the wild is rarely successful. What is needed is a change of mindset in order to co-exist with nature. In promotional literature, video and film, zoos around the world proudly proclaim their commitment to "conservation" through the captive propagation of endangered species and their eventual re-introduction to the wild. High profile animals such as golden lion tamarins, black-footed ferrets, and a few others, are routinely heralded as examples of why "modern" zoos are now important conservers of wildlife. But is re-introduction really an effective conservation vehicle? How many animals have acually been "re-introduced" and how have they fared? Are the claims of zoos to be taken seriously? This chapter looks behind the re-introduction façade and exposes the myths and challenges faced in this enormously complex endeavour.

The Hustain Nuru region of Mongolia's Chentai Mountains is one of the country's most pristine wild areas. Valleys and slopes harbour steppe vegetation such as fescue, brome grass and feathergrasses, while birch woods grow in the upper elevations of this relatively low lying mountainous region. A diverse range of wild fauna including marmots, lemmings, red deer, wild sheep, polecats, Pallas's cat, lynx and wolves call the Hustain Nuru home.

In an effort to conserve the biodiversity of this region, the Mongolian government initiated several measures to minimize human impact in the area including a prohibition on hunting and the grazing of domestic livestock. They were preparing for the return of one of Mongolia's largest native mammal species, the Przewlaski's horse, a low-slung, stocky equid with a thick neck, bristly erect mane and dorsal stripe.

In June 1992, sixteen captive-born Przewalski's horses, one of the last truly extant wild horse's of modern times, arrived in the Mongolian capital city of Ulan Bator. The horses were quickly transported by truck to Hustain Nuru, approximately 115 kilometres distant, where they were kept in 45–65 hectare enclosures; step one in their preparation for life in the wild.

Almost a year earlier, and halfway around the world, the much smaller, but equally famous black-footed ferret was taking its first tentative step back onto the wild short-grass prairie of Wyoming in the United States.

Short and mid-grass prairie once covered an enormous expanse of North America from Mexico to Canada, providing a suitable environment for untold millions of prairie dogs and hundreds of thousands of black-footed ferrets, one of their principle predators. Yet in a little more than a century, human development of the prairies and a widespread prairie dog eradication campaign resulted in the virtual elimination of black-footed ferrets.

The Wyoming project involved 49 cage-raised ferrets who were released with considerable preparation though whether or not they could survive was unknown at the time.

Re-introduction of captive-bred animals to the wild is an appealing concept that would seem, at first glance, to be a viable solution to the many problems facing endangered wildlife today.

In printed literature, video and film, zoos around the world have capitalized on this appeal. Proclaiming their commitment to the conservation of wildlife, they proudly publicize their participation in captive propagation programmes and their support for the re-introduction of endangered species back into the wild. As part of the "modern ark," they claim their efforts are saving endangered species from extinction and restoring wild animal populations.

But what are the realities of captive breeding and re-introduction? Does the zoo-going public really have an understanding of what they are supporting? Are zoos and aquariums deluding both themselves and their visitors? Do they really believe they have the answer? Are they creating a dangerous complacency, leading the public to believe that zoos are taking care of the problems faced by endangered wildlife?

According to Welfare Guidelines for the Re-Introduction of Captive Bred Mammals to the Wild (1992), published by the Universities Federation for Animal Welfare (UFAW), re-introduction is defined as "the release of animals into areas in their historical ranges where they have become extinct in the wild".

The 1987 International Union for the Conservation of Nature (IUCN) position statement, "Translocation of living organisms", provides the following definition:

In a little more than a century, human development of the prairies in the United States was responsible for the virtual elimination of the black-footed ferret

> Re-introduction of an organism, which is the intentional movement of an organism into a part of its native range from which it disappeared or became extirpated in historic times as a result of human activity or natural catastrophe.

While several slightly different definitions can be found in the literature, for the purposes of this discussion, re-introduction will be defined as the release of captive-bred or wild-caught animals into areas they no longer inhabit or in which their numbers have been seriously depleted within their historical range.

Rationales for re-introduction include the restoration of a more natural ecosystem balance through the introduction of extirpated species, to bolster an existing wildlife population by increasing numbers, and increasing their vitality through the introduction of new genetic material.

Introduction, as opposed to re-introduction, involves the release of animals into areas they have not inhabited in the past. Many introductions, both intentional and accidental have had detrimental consequences to native wildlife and habitat. Examples include the introduction of rats and domesticated cats to island ecosystems around the world resulting in the decline, extirpation, or extinction of many endemic island wildlife species. Starlings, originally released in the 1800s, now number in the millions in North America increasing competition for nesting sites with native bird species such as the eastern bluebird. Zebra mussels in the North American great lakes, rice eels in the waterways of the American Southeast, wild pigs in Hawaii, rabbits in Australia, and exotic ungulates in New Zealand are just a few of the many thousands of examples of introduced animals wreaking havoc with local species.

Translocation, in some cases referred to as re-introduction, is the transfer of animals from one location to another. This process is often carried out to re-establish a species in an area it once inhabited by drawing individuals from a stable, wild population for translocation to another location within its historic range, or to enhance numbers of an existing wild population with specimens from a separate population. Occasionally, translocation has a recreational or commercial incentive such as increasing the number of animals available for human harvest.

While there is little dispute that captive propagation and re-introduction, within a very narrow set of parameters, can be a valid component of an overall conservation strategy, the inherent difficulties of re-introduction preclude it as a tool in most instances. There is a great deal of dispute about the role of zoos in re-introduction. So far, zoos have had only a modest, and in some cases insignificant, involvement in re-introduction efforts, yet, as an industry, they have grossly overstated their own importance in this area, often for self-serving reasons.

In some regions, "slum" zoos comprise a significant percentage, sometimes 90% or more, of the "zoo industry"

Many of the re-introduction programme descriptions that follow relate to the initiatives of a few of the "better-known" zoos, as well as to those programmes administered by various governmental wildlife agencies. In describing and debating the merits of those efforts, the reader should be aware that a significant portion, possibly as high as 95% or more, of the world-wide zoo industry does not participate in, or make any attempt to participate in, recognized captive propagation and re-introduction initiatives.

While many established zoos pay only token attention to conservation, other zoos and zoo-type facilities do even less. In Canada, the United States and many other countries around the world, slum zoos, substandard wildlife exhibits, private menageries, and speciality displays abound. In some regions these facilities comprise a significant percentage, sometimes 90% or more, of the "zoo industry." Despite the fact that many "reputable" zoos try to distance themselves from these types of facilities, they exist nonetheless and should not be ignored in discussions of zoo industry activities. Looking at only the top 5–10% of zoos provides an overly sanitized view of the real situation.

With few exceptions, zoos around the world trumpet the virtues of captive propagation and re-introduction programmes. Yet few actually participate in them in a substantive way. According to David Hancocks, former executive director of the Arizona-Sonora Desert Museum:

> There is a commonly held misconception that zoos are not only saving wild animals from extinction but also reintroducing them to their wild habitats. The confusion stems from many sources, all of them zoo-based . . . In reality, most zoos

have had no contact of any kind with any re-introduction program.

Even many of the high profile Species Survival Plan (SSP) breeding programmes administered by the American Zoo and Aquarium Association (AZAA), and their counterpart programmes in other parts of the world, have no mechanism for the return of animals to the wild. And virtually all of these programmes include the maintenance of captive populations in perpetuity.

"Re-introduction is not the primary reason for captive breeding," says Michael Hutchins, director of conservation and science for the American Zoo and Aquarium Association. One of the purposes of captive propagation is to maintain captive populations of charismatic animals or "flagship species" so that zoos can raise money for conservation projects in their country of origin.

Yet many members of the public firmly believe that the goal of zoo-based captive breeding is to replenish wild animal populations and that once that is done, there will be no reason to confine those animals further.

Contrary to popular belief, most re-introduction programmes have not been initiated by zoos. Instead, they are the initiatives of government wildlife agencies, particularly in regions where these agencies are better staffed and funded, such as North America, Europe and Australia.

Many critics agree that zoos have played a legitimate, albeit small, role in re-introduction efforts, but they question the level of involvement given the resources at hand. The collective annual budget of zoos world-wide is estimated to be in the neighbourhood of 4–6 billion dollars.

Benjamin Beck, Associate Director of Biological Programs at the National Zoological Park in Washington, D.C., was able to identify only 129 re-introduction programmes, since the turn of the century, in which the origin of the animals could be determined. Despite the preponderance of zoos, numbering in the thousands world-wide, zoo-bred animals have been involved in only 76 (59%) of the programmes he identified. While stating his support for this contribution, Beck says, "Nevertheless, it does not appear that zoos are the primary proponents, animal providers, funders, or managers of re-introduction programs."

In certain cases, the motivation behind zoos' participation in captive propagation and re-introduction is suspect as well. As societal attitudes change, zoos increasingly become the targets of criticism, especially with regard to animal welfare and conservation. Are some zoos jumping on the "conservation bandwagon" in response to critics?

Many Canadian roadside zoo operators, responding to concerns about substandard conditions, erroneously claim they are involved in saving endangered species through captive breeding. Further, they state that the progeny of their animals can be, or will be, put back into the wild. Yet few of these facilities are involved in recognized captive propagation or re-introduction initiatives, and many do not even know such organized programmes exist. Even if they did, they typically don't have the resources or expertise to participate. These zoos and others like them are trying to exploit public interest in "conservation" for self-serving purposes.

Re-introduction programmes for most species are enormously complex and expensive. Even if zoos wanted to participate as full and equal partners, few have the material or financial capacity to do so. Collectively, zoos world-wide have enormous resources at hand, but little seems to actually be available for conservation work. For this reason, most zoos are peripheral players. They participate in zoo-based captive propagation initiatives in the hope that they have relevance to re-introduction efforts and conservation.

Most re-introduction programmes are complicated and expensive, involving a multi-disciplinary approach to problem solving. Long-term financial commitment, active collaboration with a broad range of public and private agencies, and an extended period of post-release follow-up, in some cases for many years, are critical to their success. This is beyond the ability of all but the best-funded zoos or zoo consortiums.

Re-introduction is not a viable strategy for the disposition of most captive animals. In fact, if it is not done properly, it can be counter-productive. In *Wild Mammals in Captivity, Principles and Techniques*, Devra Kleiman states,

> attempts to reintroduce a species, if poorly conceived or implemented, may actually obscure the conservation issues that led to the decline of the species in the first place – and thus may detract from, rather than add to, a species' chances of survival. (IUCN 1987)

In addition to the difficulties of gathering sufficient support for re-introduction programmes, other obstacles exist. For the purposes of this discussion, these additional factors have been divided into two broad categories:

1. Environmental/biological
2. Human-caused

In determining whether or not a re-introduction programme is a viable conservation strategy, certain criteria must be satisfied. Environmental, biological and human-based factors may all impact re-introduction efforts. Human-based factors are discussed in the following section.

ENVIRONMENTAL/BIOLOGICAL FACTORS AFFECTING RE-INTRODUCTION

One criterion that must be satisfied is the availability of suitable habitat. In order to determine whether or not a potential release site is suitable, it must be thoroughly studied and analysed. Do the conditions that threatened the original population or its habitat still exist? If they do, can their impact be mitigated sufficiently for re-introduction to succeed?

Environmental changes (i.e. altered weather patterns, modification of forest type, reduction in water levels, human development, etc.) which may impact re-introduction efforts may have occurred at potential release sites. The longer the release candidate has been absent from the site, the greater the likelihood that environmental changes have occurred. If a species has been absent from its original habitat for a relatively brief period, changes that have occurred may be minor and inconsequential. However, for a species that has not been extant in its historical range for decades or centuries, conditions may have changed substantially. For example, if the survival of a bird species was dependent on intact stands of old growth forest, it wouldn't do any good to introduce individuals of that species into newer second or third growth forest areas.

The World Zoo Conservation Strategy (1994) outlines two factors pertaining to the return of *ex situ* populations to damaged habitat:

> the complexity of the original biotope, and the complexity of the relationships of the species within its natural surroundings. Species which originally lived in complex environments and had complex interactions may not be able to return to the wild after total disappearance of their biotope. Nonetheless, species with less complex relationships, or living in a less complex habitat have a much better chance.

A second important criterion is the need for a stable, self-sustaining captive population from which individuals can be drawn for re-introduction purposes. The population must be sufficiently robust so that the removal, and subsequent loss, of "surplus" reintroduced individuals over an extended period of time will not severely impact on the genetic integrity of the captive population. In cases where the population is reduced to near extinction levels, it may not be possible to satisfy this criterion.

Because re-introduction protocols are still, for the most part, experimental, they are constantly evolving. Many release initiatives experience a high level of mortality, so the number of individuals withdrawn from the ex situ population may be high. As release protocols are refined, it is hoped that there will be a corresponding increase in the survivorship of released individuals.

The small number of individuals within many ex situ populations

© Zoocheck Canada Inc.

Animals that have been bred in captivity must be thoroughly prepared if they are to be successfully released into the wild

and the inability of animals to choose their own breeding partners (for the most part, pairings are predicated on a "scientifically-based" human decision making process) create concerns about inbreeding depression. Will the physical traits which allow animals to successfully exploit specific environments in the wild still be intact in potential release candidates? Will lack of genetic variability lead to deterioration of the ex situ population?

In the wild, individuals with superior abilities stand the greatest chance of long-term survival, reaching sexual maturity and passing their genes on to future generations. In captivity, most animals receive total institutional care. They do not require the same skills and physical traits that their wild counterparts require. Undesirable attributes may be carried forward from generation to generation because natural selection is not playing a part.

Being ill-equipped, both physically and behaviourally, to survive in a wild environment is a major hurdle that must be overcome by each species in all re-introduction attempts. Potential release candidates must know how to avoid predators; find food and shelter; travel; navigate; and associate with conspecifics in a normal fashion.

One of the highest profile examples of insufficient physical ability involves Keiko the orca whale of Free Willy fame. Keiko is currently undergoing a process of physical and behavioural rehabilitation aimed at increasing his chance of survival upon release into the Atlantic Ocean.

After years of living in cramped quarters in aquariums in Canada and Mexico, Keiko was grossly underweight and able to submerge for only a few minutes at a time. His lack of fitness would have almost certainly been a death warrant should he have been returned to the wild unprepared.

Upon being moved to a larger, more modern facility in the United States, Keiko gradually gained weight and increased his fitness level, substantially increasing the duration of his dives. With proper preparation and training, it is hoped that Keiko, who now resides in a sea pen off the coast of Iceland, may soon have a chance to survive and prosper with his counterparts in the wild.

Pre-release preparation for most captive-bred animals is critical to their survival in the wild. Nothing can be taken for granted. Even basic activities such as moving about may reveal never before experienced hazards for captive-bred specimens.

Arguably the most famous re-introduction subject is the golden-lion tamarin, a tiny monkey that once inhabited substantial regions of Brazilian coastal rainforest. With the demise of suitable forest habitat, a reduction of more than 90%, the golden-lion tamarin in the wild now exists only as a remnant population of a few hundred individuals in the Poco das Antas Biological Reserve.

Observations of initial releases demonstrated an inability on the part of captive-bred tamarins to locomote through the forest as their wild counterparts did – a skill essential to their survival. To address this inability, the National Zoological Park in Washington, D.C., now puts potential release candidates into a naturally forested segment of the zoo where they can learn to leap, climb, and travel normally. The Duke University Primate Centre in Durham, North Carolina, is another facility in which captive-bred primates learn to climb and locomote, forage for food, and become aware of natural dangers in a forest environment during pre-release training. It is worth noting that both of these situations bear little resemblance to standard types of zoo displays.

Behavioural competence is critical to the successful release of most captive-bred animals, especially for socially complex species. While some animals, such as many invertebrate species, seem to rely heavily on hard-wired, instinctual behaviours, others, such as wolves, bears, elephants and apes, learn a good deal of their natural behavioural regime from conspecifics over an extended period of time.

Ensuring that release subjects are behaviourally competent is difficult because so little is known about the natural behavioural regimes of many species. Says Devra Kleiman in *Wild Mammals in Captivity, Principles and Techniques*,

We do not know which of these behaviours are learned and thus require training, and which are genetically hard-wired.

>

In *Przewalski's Horse, the History and Biology of an Endangered Species*, Lee Boyd and Katherine A. Houpt state,

The behaviour of a species is often one of the last areas of their

> biology to be studied and one of the last aspects to be considered in making management decisions.

David Hancocks comments on zoos specifically,

> The spaces in which animals are displayed in zoos are rarely tolerable for sustaining natural behaviours. The regime under which zoos maintain their animals in no way prepares their skills for survival.

For a great many species, social preparation is also critically important, especially when the introduction is meant to supplement an existing wild population. If introduced specimens are unable to interact in an appropriate manner with wild individuals, conflict can result. Captive-bred specimens may have had little or no opportunity to acquire cultural or traditional behaviour patterns and may be additionally disadvantaged when released.

> Types of behaviours that often have cultural components in birds include song dialects, alarm calls, foraging techniques, mobbing behaviour, and locations of migratory routes and breeding sites. (Bonner 1980; Mondinger 1980)

> For animals with learned behaviour, loss of 'culture' may pose the most significant barrier to successful re-introductions.

Cultural behaviours have also been noted in primate, elephant and cetacean species.

Failure to achieve the desired level of preparedness for release candidates has hindered the progress of many re-introduction efforts. Examples include captive-raised chimpanzees lacking the necessary social abilities required for integration into wild groups; red wolves lacking the necessary flight response to danger; captive-bred black-footed ferrets lacking the ability to hunt, kill and consume prairie dogs; and hand-reared thick-billed parrots failing to recognize avian predators.

Another critical consideration in any re-introduction effort is the possibility that a previously unknown disease organism may be introduced from captive-bred specimens to an existing wild population, with potentially catastrophic effects.

In 1991, the prestigious National Zoological Park in Washington, D.C. was making final preparations for the shipment of eleven golden-lion tamarins to Brazil where they would be released into the wild. Three days before their departure, blood tests indicated that one of the monkeys carried an antibody to a lethal virus which had recently claimed the lives of more than 40 tamarins in a number of US zoos. The virus in question was called an arenavirus – a deadly pathogen that can spread rapidly within the species. Prior to the blood test, the monkey showed no signs of illness.

If the virus had gone undetected, it may have been introduced into South America, where it does not exist, and wrought havoc with the wild golden-lion tamarin population and possibly other primate species as well.

According to National Zoological Park associate director of biological programmes, Benjamin Beck, "It's a very serious potential problem. It's only because of our advanced facilities that we were able to catch this virus. Who knows what else is going through?"

With a broad range of species in a relatively confined setting and a preponderance of rats, mice and cockroaches to serve as carriers, zoos are potential hotbeds for disease. Making things even worse is the fact that many diseases are in a state of constant evolution, changing rapidly to keep ahead of their hosts, making complete screening difficult, if not impossible.

According to wildlife veterinarian, Michael Woodford, "Zoo-bred stock is often exposed to exotic pathogens brought in from foreign countries and to infections transmitted by attendants and visitors. Furthermore, captivity subjects some species to continual stress, resulting in immunodepression and increased susceptibility to infection."

Herpetologist Clifford Warwick is also concerned about transmission of disease, stating "Introduction of pathological conditions to nature may be easily initiated. For example, it seems that a significant cause of disease and mortality among free-living American tortoises may be attributable to occasional releases of infected former pet animals."

Even the most carefully executed programmes can suffer unexpected outbreaks of disease. In 1986, fifty-seven predominantly captive-born Arabian oryx were transferred from the collection of the late King Khaled of Saudi Arabia near Riyadh to the National Wildlife Research Centre in Taif, approximately 600 miles away. The animals were selected as possible candidates for release into the wild. Several of the oryx soon became sick and died of acute tuberculosis. It's believed that the stress of being moved played a part in the outbreak.

A second generation oryx herd comprized of hand-reared tuberculosis-free animals was then established to produce offspring for release purposes. It is hoped that tuberculosis will not surface again in Saudi Arabian oryx.

To ensure, as best they can, that release candidates are free from unwanted parasites and disease organisms, zoo and re-introduction personnel quarantine and test animals prior to shipment to their destination locations. Many are also subject to quarantining upon arrival, and a complete veterinary screening before release. However, even with these safeguards in place, the risk is tangible.

In "Welfare Guidelines for the Re-Introduction of Captive Bred

Mammals to the Wild" (UFAW, 1992), the stated aim of re-introduction includes health and disease considerations, "The aim in reintroducing captive reared mammals into the wild is to establish a viable population of the species in an area in a way that does not constitute a physical or health hazard to local human or animal populations."

Severely endangered wild populations should not be allowed to mix with captive-bred specimens, unless the addition of new genetic material is critical to their survival.

HUMAN FACTORS AFFECTING RE-INTRODUCTION

The political side of wildlife re-introduction is often complex, controversial, and difficult to resolve. One of the highest profile examples of the ramifications of politics on re-introduction is the recent release of wolves into various parts of the United States, including the world-renowned Yellowstone National Park, an area which the wolves historically inhabited but from which they were extirpated many years ago.

The lobby against the wolf re-introduction programme was large, well organized and vocal. Ranchers concerned about their livestock, misinformed members of the public, and anti-environmental organizations, all spoke out against the programme.

In the *Wolves of Yellowstone, The Inside Story*, author Douglas W. Smith talks about the opposition, "The climate at the time the first wolves arrived in 1995 was uncertain at best. The controversy surrounding the re-introduction had reached a crescendo. Three lawsuits were filed trying to stop the re-introduction, even as the wolves were en route to Yellowstone." Whether or not wolves will prosper in Yellowstone and the surrounding regions is still unknown.

The Mexican grey wolf recovery programme faced similar opposition. Of eleven wolves released into the Apache National Forest in eastern Arizona, five have been shot, two are missing and presumed dead, and the rest were recaptured during the fall of 1998 to ensure their survival. Since that time, two additional pairs of wolves, with hindquarters spray – painted orange in the hope that they will not be shot, have been released.

One of the major obstacles to the highly publicized red wolf recovery programme has been the difficulty in finding a politically safe habitat for the wolves. After a seemingly successful effort to establish red wolves in the Alligator River National Wildlife Refuge in North Carolina, 37 red wolves were released in the Great Smoky Mountain National Park in Tennessee. Most of them didn't survive very long or had to be captured when they strayed beyond the boundaries of the park. In October 1998, the eight-year Great Smoky Mountain red wolf recovery effort ended with the capture of the last surviving wolves.

The political will to protect habitat over the long term is a critical factor in the success of re-introductions. Governments must not only be willing to set aside suitable habitat for wildlife, they must also be willing to commit the necessary resources to provide effective, on-the-ground protection for it. In some cases, like those mentioned above, even that wasn't enough.

Social factors must also be considered in the development and implementation of re-introduction programmes. Many animals, including most fish, bird and grazing mammal species generate little concern. They don't compete with humans, kill domesticated live-stock, and are not generally considered dangerous. Others, however, such as large carnivores, like the wolves mentioned previously, may be seen as competing with local human interests and may be incorrectly perceived as dangerous. If possible, these concerns must be addressed.

Re-introduction programmes should, where possible, also provide tangible benefit to the local human population. While most people understand and share concern over the loss of wildlife and wild habitat, practical human concerns often lead to conflict situations. For example, poor communities bordering wildlife reserves or parks may rely on illegal poaching of wildlife to supplement their protein needs, or they may collect fuel-wood, damaging critical habitat and causing disturbance in the process. These activities may have a severe impact on re-introduction initiatives. To ensure re-introduction success, the needs of local communities must be considered and co-operation obtained. If no incentive for co-operation exists, the chances of the re-introduction effort succeeding are diminished. Ideally, local communities should also be involved in the implementation of the re-introduction.

In *Wild Mammals in Captivity, Principles and Techniques*, Devra Kleiman states:

> Conservationists need to be sensitive to the pressures affecting the activities of local individuals, especially government officials, so that the latter are not put in impossible or compromising positions due to the activities of the re-introduction programme . . . [T]he politics of re-introduction are as important as the release methodology . . . A good re-introduction programme involves local collaborators with a stake in its future success.

The release of captive-bred Arabian oryx, a strikingly beautiful desert antelope with long scimitar-like horns, into Oman is one of the better known examples of a re-introduction programme which has involved and benefited local people. The Harasis tribespeople who inhabit the region in which the oryx were released serve as oryx protectors and receive compensation for doing so. Not surprisingly, this is considered by many to be one of the most successful re-introductions to date. However, during the last decade poaching of live animals to be sold as breeding animals has caused considerable concern and may turn success into failure.

Anyone reviewing the literature produced by zoos world-wide would inevitably be led to conclude that the "modern ark" is saving innumerable wildlife species from extinction and restoring them to their wild habitats. But the literature, often produced by zoo marketing and publicity departments, is misleading. While a few species have been assisted, the "modern ark" isn't really doing what many people think it is.

Zoo hyperbole aside, re-introduction is not a panacea. At best re-introduction is a viable strategy in the conservation of only a tiny number of species. According to Benjamin Beck, "We can find evidence that only 16 (11%) of the 145 re-introduction projects contributed to the establishment of a self-sustaining wild population. These sixteen projects reintroduced captive-born wood bison, plains bison, Arabian oryx, Alpine ibex, bald eagle, Harris' hawk, peregrine falcon, Aleutian goose, bean goose, lesser white-fronted goose, wood duck, masked bobwhite quail, Galapagos iguana, pine snake, and Galapagos tortoise." Many of these examples are translocations into previously occupied or vacant habitat, and were not pivotal to the survival of the species.

While Beck also outlines how re-introduction efforts can be valuable in other ways, he acknowledges that "at this point . . . there is not overwhelming evidence that re-introduction is successful".

Yet zoos the world over proudly proclaim the success of their efforts to save endangered species through captive breeding and re-introduction, repeatedly highlighting the releases of a small number of species such as golden-lion tamarins and California condors.

But critics argue that while a very small number of species may have been assisted by zoo-based captive propagation and re-introduction efforts, the contribution of the industry as a whole in this regard is pathetically minuscule when compared to the resources they command.

The release of captive-bred oryx into Oman not only helped to establish a wild population but also helped the local people, who received compensation for acting as their protectors

According to the World Zoo Conservation Strategy (WZCS), "If all institutions under a broad definition of zoos (i.e., exhibiting wild, or non-domestic, animals to the public) are included, then the total number of zoos in the world may be well over 10,000. The number of zoos world-wide participating in national, regional, or international zoo federations is approximately 1,000." The strategy also states that the thousand or so zoos in organized networks "annually receive at least 600 million visitors, this being over 10% of the entire world population".

In fact the estimate of 10,000 zoos may be low. In many countries, accurate records of zoos don't exist. In Canada, less than 30 zoos are accredited members of the Canadian Association of Zoos and Aquariums, the industry's national association, while an additional 20 or so participate in the organization as non-voting affiliate members. Yet investigative work by Zoocheck Canada has revealed hundreds of additional facilities, many of them slum zoos, private menageries, and speciality displays. Several years ago, a Born Free Foundation investigation known as the European Survey of Zoos resulted in a list of nearly 1,000 zoo facilities in that region alone, a great many of them previously unknown outside of their local area.

Based on the WZCS estimate of 10,000 zoos, the World Society for the Protection of Animals and the Born Free Foundation place the annual global zoo budget in the neighbourhood of $4–$6 billion dollars. These thousands of facilities employ tens of thousands of workers who spend tens of millions of hours tending, managing and marketing millions of individual animals in zoos around the world.

Yet despite this enormous base of resources, only 16 successful re-introductions have been achieved, most of them not being zoo-based initiatives. If we accept Benjamin Beck's contention that many other of the 145 re-introduction programmes have been assisted by zoos, this contribution still seems negligible in the scheme of things. And this is the most striking criticism against the captive propagation and re-introduction claims of the zoo industry.

Finally, we must compare the costs of zoo-based captive propagation and re-introduction versus the cost of in situ conservation. Is it possible that the resources put into these activities would be better spent directly protecting wild habitats and the multitude of species they shelter?

The Zoo Inquiry (1994) provides a financial comparison of in situ versus ex situ black rhino conservation. It states that the "annual captive maintenance of black rhino per animal" is $16,800, while the "annual cost of protecting appropriate wild habitat to support one rhino" is $1,000. It goes on, "It has been estimated that it can cost 100 times more to maintain a group of elephants in captivity for a year than to conserve a similar group, and their entire ecosystem, in situ for the same period."

The 492,000 hectare Garamba National Park in Zaire operates at an annual cost of $269,500, close to the estimated annual cost of keeping sixteen black rhino in captivity. Yet Garamba National Park protects an entire ecosystem that is home to 31 northern white rhino, 4,000 elephant, 30,000 buffalo, the entire giraffe population of Zaire, 14 other ungulate species, 16 carnivore species, 10 primate species, and 98 small mammal species.

Many zoo critics concede that there may be a role, albeit a small one, for zoo-based captive propagation and re-introduction initiatives. However, the effectiveness of that role will be greatly diminished if the current level of misspent energy and resources, that ultimately does nothing to save wildlife and wild habitat, continues.

Zoo proponents argue that the conservation contribution of zoos will improve in the future, that captive propagation and re-introduction is a new and evolving science, and that zoos contribute to conservation in many other ways. Regardless of whether or not these arguments are true, the record to date speaks for itself. Compared to the resources they command, the world-wide zoo community has not made a substantial contribution to wildlife conservation through captive propagation and re-introduction.

At a time when the current rate of extinction is estimated to be 50,000 species per year or six per hour, is the glacially slow, single species management approach to conservation practised by zoos really going to work? The Przewalski's horse and black-footed ferret are not yet self-sustaining in the wild. Perhaps at some point in the future, they will be. Will zoos be able to make the difference they so feverishly prophesy? For the animals' sake, I hope so, but I'm not holding my breath.

References

Anderson, Christopher, "Keeping new zoo diseases out of the wild, Deadly 'emerging virus' in Tamarin monkeys reveals danger of re-introduction campaigns. In *Washington Post*, 1991.

Born Free Foundation/WSPA, The Zoo Inquiry, UK, 1994.

Brooke, James, "Jungle reserve in Brazil bringing rare primate back from brink". In *New York Times*.

Boyd, Houpt, *Przewalski's Horse, The History and Biology of an Endangered Species*. New York: State University of New York Press, 1994.

Croke, Vicki, *The Modern Ark, The Story of Zoos: Past, Present and Future*. New York: Scribner, 1997.

Derr, Mark, "As rescue plan for threatened species, breeding programs falter". In *New York Times*, 1999.

Gibbons, Edward F., Durrant, Barbara S. and Demarest, Jack, eds, *Conservation of Endangered Species in Captivity, An Interdisciplinary Approach*. New York: State University of New York Press, 1995.

Haring, David, *The Right Stuff, In Wildlife Conservation*. New York: Wildlife Conservation Society, April 1999.

International Academy of Animal Welfare Sciences, *Welfare Guidelines For the Re-Introduction of Captive Bred Mammals to the Wild*. Universities Federation for Animal Welfare, 1992.

IUDZG/CBSG (IUCN/SSC), *The World Zoo Conservation Strategy*. Chicago: Chicago Zoological Society, 1993.
Harris, Holly, (Managing Editor); Devra G. Kleiman, Mary E. Allen, Katerina V. Thompson and Susan Lumpkin, eds, *Re-introduction Programs, Wild Mammals in Captivity, Principles and Techniques*. Chicago: University of Chicago Press, 1997.
Lee, David N. B., "Mexican wolf killed, conservation hotline", in *Wildlife Conservation*. New York: Wildlife Conservation Society, April 1999.
Lee, David N. B., "Red Wolf recovery ends in the Smokies, conservation hotline", in *Wildlife Conservation*. New York: Wildlife Conservation Society, April 1999.
Miller, Brian, Reading, Richard P. and Forrest, Steve, *Prairie Night, Black-Footed Ferrets and the Recovery of Endangered Species*. Washington D.C.: Smithsonian Institution Press, 1996.
Norton Hutchins and Stevens Maple, eds, *Ethics on the Ark, Zoos, Animal Welfare and Wildlife Conservation*. Washington, D.C.: Smithsonian Institution Press, 1995.
Smith, Phillips, *The Wolves of Yellowstone, the Inside Story*. Stillwater, Minnesota: Voyageur Press, 1996.
Tudge, Colin, *Last Animals at the Zoo*. Hutchinson Radius, 1991.
Wiese, Hutchins, *Species Survival Plans, Strategies for Wildlife Conservation*, Alexandria: American Zoo and Aquarium Association, 1994.
Woodford, Rossiter, "Disease risks associated with wildlife translocation projects". Rev. sci. tech. Off. int. Epiz., 1993, 12(1): 115–35.

6 Understanding Human Responses to Endangered Species

Samantha Scott

The way in which human beings respond to the plight of endangered species depend on many factors. That they do respond is vital for the continued efforts in conservation to be sustained. Understanding why people respond to some schemes more enthusiastically than others is important in targeting and maintaining interest and funding in key areas of conservation. This chapter discusses what people understand by the term "endangered species", how they may think it effects them and the world at large and what is being done to save them. It looks at ex situ versus in situ conservation projects and the moral and practical arguments of both.

A human response, be it considered or immediate, to any given issue is governed by a myriad of a factors.

First, there are our inherent prejudices and belief systems about the issue. These will have been formed by associations made at times when we were impressionable, which usually, and perhaps sadly, means when we were young. Trailing around the zoo on wet, miserable days with a bored teacher will have done nothing to foster good feelings for such institutions. However, if the zoo were a romantic trysting place, our associations may be somewhat more favourable. In terms of education, if we were told as schoolchildren that conservation equals zoos equals a Good Thing, and there was nothing to challenge that view, then the chances are that the majority of us would accept this into our belief system. Later on, conflicting evidence may challenge that belief and it would depend upon our level of interest and the immediacy of the issue for us whether or not we could be bothered to rethink that belief as a single viewpoint rather than as an axiom.

Secondly, there is the profile and the bias which the media places on the issue. Whether or not it is a topic which we would describe as "close to our hearts", it is difficult not to subconsciously absorb and assimilate headlines, snatches of news, documentaries and colleagues' and friends' interpretation of the same.

Thirdly, our level of knowledge about the issue determines whether our opinions will be informed or whether they will be a mish-mash result of the first two factors. Unless (and sometimes despite) that knowledge is derived from personal experience, there is a tendency to take on board the inherent prejudice of those presenting the information, be it via television documentaries, news items, journalists, animal welfare groups, zoo directors – the authors of this book! It takes a clinical and analytical mind to be able to read and watch well crafted arguments without veering from one camp to the other as firstly one then the opposite point of view is persuasively put forward by the proponents of each.

Fourthly, the prominence which we give these issues in our minds will depend upon what other events – personal, local, global – are impinging upon our consciousness and, indeed, consciences at any given time.

Fifthly, cultural influences can play an important part in the credence and prominence we give to issues. Animal issues are no exception to this. Religion, spiritual belief and irreligious conviction in the superiority of man over animals, as well as superstitions and the never-to-be-underestimated power of fashion can, and do, have vast implications for the likelihood of succeeding in bringing an issue to the forefront of peoples' minds.

Animal issues, because they concern other sentient beings, who are vulnerable and reliant on man's actions for their well-being and future, have the potential for arousing powerful, and sometimes conflicting, responses in individuals, within groups of individuals and between cultures and countries. Within the issue of conservation and endangered species, the problem of understanding those responses becomes more complex – because conservation is about more than whether or not we allow a certain species to suffer or to die out. It carries implications for the environment, for other species and for human populations, not only for the present and for our immediate future, but for the world's future. Such topics spark reactions which range from the fatalistic to the impassioned and occasionally fanatical, but almost everyone has a view, based as it may be on any or all of the above criteria.

As always, responses of corporate bodies come into play from the organizations whose remits claim an environmental/conservationist interest, but who may not actually agree with each other, to the multinationals who have recognized that such issues are of importance to the consumer/shareholder and who purport to share these concerns by their logos and in their business practice. It is, of course, up to the individual to discern the difference between altruistic interest, merely jumping on the bandwagon of popular opinion, or, worse, merely paying lip service to the issue.

It remains a fact, however, that such organizations have tremendous power in conservation issues, because of their money, their locations, their influence on local prosperity and because of their immediate effects on the local flora and fauna. These may be effected grossly and obviously by devastation and landscape change; more insidiously, but importantly, by pollution, cultural influences and economic changes both locally and nationally.

In trying to understand human responses to endangered species, we need to address the following questions:

- What do people understand by "Endangered Species" and how do they think this effects them if at all?
- What do people understand is being done to help save these species?
- How important are zoos versus "in situ" conservation projects?
- What are the moral arguments of the above? And the practical ones?
- What impact is it perceived that the various schemes are making on world populations ?

Some of these questions will have been dealt with in other chapters, but it is necessary to touch upon them here since they are pivotal to how people respond to the issue of conservation. And unless we can understand how and why these responses occur we are never likely to progress beyond being disparate and squabbling groups and cultures with nothing much left to squabble about.

WHAT IS UNDERSTOOD BY "ENDANGERED SPECIES"?

Many people have an understanding that certain species in the world are rapidly disappearing. The overall perception of the problem tends to lay the blame on the encroachment of man, of "civilization", of multinational corporations on the remaining wild areas of the world, forcing animal species into more confined and limited habitats and on the perceived (but often incorrect) "fact" that other governments are not doing enough or caring enough about the problems. Many people also have some sort of impression of the vast scale of slaughter which has seen the decimation of the elephant, tiger and rhino population by poaching.

The extent of the problem, its implications for the future and the vast political and legal network enmeshing the struggle for solutions, are probably beyond what most people not directly involved in conservation could begin to appreciate. This is not surprising: conservation is not a "user friendly" issue as we shall see; the public at large are not culpable for their limited grasp of the situation.

The Convention on International Trade in Endangered Species (CITES)[1] aims to protect those species threatened with extinction (i.e. endangered) by controlling trade in those species or parts of thereof.

In addition to CITES, individual countries deal with their own at-risk species and their protection may not be limited to trade restrictions. For example, The Committee on the Status of Endangered Wildlife in Canada defines "endangered" with specific reference to

Canada and the Canadian provinces and is taken to be: "Any indigenous species of fauna or flora that is threatened with imminent extinction or extirpation throughout all or a significant portion of its Canadian range."[2] By this definition, already the wolf, wolverine, polar bear, grizzly and cougar are in danger or vulnerable, yet to see the number of cougars and wolves in appalling conditions in roadside zoos in, particularly, Ontario, the public could be misled into thinking they are plentiful and far from endangered.

In the opening paragraph of the CITES document the statement on behalf of the contracting states begins that, by agreeing to abide by the terms of the Convention they (the states) are:

> Recognising that the wild fauna and flora in their many beautiful and varied forms are an irreplaceable part of the natural systems of the earth which must be protected for this and generations to come . . .[3]

Despite the fact that CITES lists many of these flora and fauna as in need of protection, it tends to be the glamorous, the significantly sized, the dangerous (these are often glamorous because they are dangerous) and the appealing species which receive the most publicity and consequently the majority of the resources. No one should detract from London Zoo's successful efforts to save the Partula snail, but, ironically, it is those individuals which are large, tragic (elephant, gorilla, giraffe, panda) and ultimately unsuccessful in survival and reproduction terms which capture the public's attention. This is because the birth and death of a baby gorilla or the death of giraffe is more newsworthy, provides better copy and more scope for visual presentation than does a snail.

The impression with which many people are left is that there are a few, but significant, number of wonderful and striking creatures which need saving. This is to be achieved by money, by experts, by "captive breeding", by "preserving the gene pool" and, if we are very lucky, by saving the habitat. The latter has been deemed arguably the most difficult objective to achieve: conflict, politics, access, competition for space and resources with locals and with international corporations makes fighting for habitat an unrewarding and unglamorous job and somehow not as high a priority as breeding replacement animals.

In *Adieu to the Zoo?*[4] David Hancocks describes how, in a survey by Defenders of Wildlife (1994), zero percent of 1500 people sampled offered loss of biodiversity as one of the environmental threats to the planet. They could all volunteer problems such as loss of rainforests, the ozone layer depletion and oil spillages, presumably because these had an impact upon them through the media, but according to Communications Consortium 1994, cited in the same paper,[5] only 1 in 5 Americans claims even to have heard of biodiversity. At the same meeting, Dr Simon Lyster[6] cites one of the problems being that the media find

> the whole concept of biodiversity rather boring and difficult to explain.

It is not only the media who fail this issue: biodiversity is not an issue about which zoos educate their visitors. In fact a very skewed impression is gained by the zoo visitor of the variety of species with which we share the planet. This impression is created not only by the species which are present in zoos and which are given high profile, as outlined above, but, more significantly by those under or not represented at all in zoological collections. One example of this discrepancy[7] cites a comparison between the composition of the average American Zoo Association zoo and the species on the planet. Mammal species were represented at a ratio of 1:31, birds 1:98 and reptiles 1:104. Amphibians 91:2500 come second to a staggering 1:2.3 million for invertebrates. It is hardly surprising, therefore, that the zoo visiting public are not well informed about biodiversity and that their response to the subject of endangered species is based on a little knowledge of a very few selected species.

People need to have an understanding of what we have on the planet, what we have lost in the past and what we are losing now and are likely to lose in the future, only then can they realize that the scale of the problem extends way beyond what their faith in a few institutions can deliver, however worthy the aspirations and endeavours of those institutions may be.

In addition to the losses of which we are aware, as Douglas Adams points out in his excellent book *Last Chance to See*,[8] species (plant and animal) of which we have no knowledge are disappearing all the time. Who knows what devastating effect this may have by altering microclimates, parasitic burdens, food supply and disease?

In order that the people of the world can envisage what is at stake, it needs to be understood that the small, the ugly, the poisonous and the unglamorous; those that infest the bowels (literally) of the worlds' mammals and those that are never heard of or seen are often more important to conservation and to the ultimate protection of endangered species than the birth of a single tiger cub in captivity. It follows that some concept of the complexity of the connections between plant, animal, soil, climate and microclimate must be grasped before such an understanding can occur.

HOW DO PEOPLE SEE THAT THE ISSUE OF ENDANGERED SPECIES AFFECTS THEM, IF AT ALL?

How people think that the issue, indeed the fact of, endangered species affects them depends upon where they live, their cultural and religious attitudes, the attention which the issue is given by their education and media and how they personally view the world and its future.

It could be said that having the time to worry about endangered species is a consequence of the luxury of not having to worry about day-to-day survival, e.g. obtaining food, water and shelter and it cannot perhaps be expected of people with less privileged lifestyles to spend their time, money and energy on something which affects them (apparently) so indirectly. This argument has its validity as it stands and no one would suggest that people fighting for survival in war-torn areas of the world or those suffering the aftermath of environmental disaster should give their time and meagre resources to anything but survival. However, a counter argument would state that day-to-day life does ultimately depend upon giving the issue of endangered species (and the concomitant disappearing habitat) serious consideration and action. In his book *The Tiger's Destiny*,[9] Valmik Thapar describes how the future of the tiger and the future of Ranthambhore National Park are inextricably linked:

> the tiger's destiny cannot be separated from the uncertain destiny of our planet.

The day-to-day lives of the local people and their future depends upon the maintenance of the forest which supports the tiger.

The poachers of tigers, of rhino horn and other endangered species would undoubtedly also say that their livelihood depends upon the future of the endangered species which is their prey, but they could hardly be described as using their "resource" in a sustainable manner. Numbers of animals killed, the market price for a given animal part and avoiding being caught are the only issues to which the poacher would give immediate attention.

Superstitions, desire for the medical properties of tiger parts and for the fashionable merits of rhino horn dagger handles drive the market. This keeps poachers taking risks and drives these species closer to extinction. Such desires and fashions take higher priority in the minds of consumers in Yemen, China, Korea and Taiwan, for example, than do long-term concerns about species survival. The effects of publicity and the pressures of the western press do not make as much impact in these countries or on those markets, although targeting markets has always been stressed as the area most likely to have a major impact on poaching and trade in animal parts.

The West may now take the moral high ground with regard to such fashions, but the responsibility for damage done on a vast scale by "big game hunting" of the recent colonial past lies at its door. We should not forget that the purchase of ivory used to be fashionable in Europe and the USA and that hunting for fur to produce coats and other goods continues. Although such obvious extermination is unlikely to ever be countenanced again by the West, it should be remembered that in fifty years time the world will probably wring its hands in horror at the decimation of the planet's resources for which the West is largely responsible but towards which it is often blithely indifferent. Cultural differences in fashion and desire for animal products is not always driven by the East–West divide; fur goods are more widely displayed and sold in Canada, for instance, than they are in the UK where the animal rights lobby and stark protests have made the wearing of fur not only unfashionable but a heinous offence.

WHAT DO PEOPLE UNDERSTAND IS BEING DONE TO SAVE THESE SPECIES?

> Protecting the tiger in isolation is not the answer; the tiger's future is interwoven with the problems of diminishing natural resources and increasing human demands.[10]

This is true of all the species in question, but seeing individual animals, "representatives" of endangered species, in zoos and wildlife parks belies this fundamental truth. The implication is that by saving the species, by preserving the gene pool and maintaining numbers the battle for the future of endangered species is being won.

In general, the public tends to believe that the "experts", the zoos and wildlife parks, committed in their agenda to research and conservation, are taking the only possible route towards species survival, given the inherent problems of habitat management. These problems are perceived to be those produced by the politics of the countries involved and wars which further diminish the species numbers and create impossible risks for those working in the field. Very little understanding of the relationship between local people and the species involved is included in this perception. For example, loss of habitat for both the Indian and African elephant means that these animals impinge, in a very dramatic way, upon the lives of farmers and villagers.

Although the protection of the forest habitat is vital for protection of the tiger and ultimately for the local people, the immediate effects for these people are of restricted access to the forest from which they have always derived essential resources. In this way, resentment towards the species in question may be fostered, further inhibiting the efforts of those working towards habitat protection and in situ breeding programmes. These are very real difficulties, but they are not the all-or-nothing problems which the public imagine to be the major factors involved in *in situ* projects for species and habitat survival. The war in Rwanda disrupted the gorilla project. The staff were forced to leave though some have since returned. The media reported on the intransigence of government and the grinding slowness of political change. But the grass roots, day-to-day issues of whether the forest guards get paid, how the co-operation of the locals may be won over, and the logistical difficulties of access to medicines and moving supplies are given little attention. Yet these are the issues which ultimately make or break a project; they are difficult, but with application of resources, intelligence and compassion, by no means insurmountable.

Now, we have seen that many people are unaware of the enormity of the problem of loss of biodiversity and the relevance of the interconnections between animals and their immediate organic surroundings. It has also been described how the public have a rather skewed view of the relative amounts and importance of work being done in zoological parks and in the field. The danger of this combined misunderstanding is that the tendency is for zoos to attract funds that might otherwise go to wildlife conservation in situ. One example cited by the Wild Lands Project is that American foundations which contribute to both zoos and environmental organizations, donate far greater amounts of money to zoos.[11]

INTERNATIONAL LAW

If the understanding by the public of the international laws governing the protection of and trade in Endangered Species is hazy at best, then this may be because many governments, non-governmental organizations and even conservationists themselves are not clear on the meaning, the clout and the implications of the various agreements which exist.

Media coverage of these laws is scant; only tending to cover issues which, from journalistic experience, are known to capture the public attention (e.g. downlisting the African Elephant from CITES Appendix I to Appendix II in 1997). Appendix I prohibits trade whereas appendix II permits monitored trade.

In 1992 much publicity was given to the Rio Earth Summit and the Biodiversity Convention was signed by almost every country in the world (with the notable exception of the United States), in time for governments to show the world positive outcomes from the summit, but since that flurry of media attention, all has gone quiet in the newsrooms of the world and consequently there is little pressure on governments to implement the Convention quickly.[12]

Anyone who has been to Turkey in the last ten years and particularly to Dalyan will recall the numerous brochures handed out to tourists regarding the plight of the sea turtles on Dalyan beach. In order to accommodate both turtle and tourist there are rules about where one can walk and sunbathe so as not to disturb the turtles' nesting sites. Despite the fact that this probably increases the attraction of Dalyan to, especially, the western tourist, Turkey had to be "persuaded", under the Bern Convention and by its desire to join the European Community, to step in to protect the site.[13]

Many people have heard of CITES; once they are made aware of the existence of other laws drawn up for the protection of endangered species, they then need to understand that it is political will, public and media pressure and the persistence of conservationists and lawyers who will determine whether these laws are made to work. Just because the treaties are in place does not mean that complacency should be allowed to set in.

FACTORS FUELLING COMPLACENCY

As far as people's understanding and response to endangered species is concerned there are two main arguments regarding the contribution of zoos and wildlife parks.

The first is that, because people can see the individual animal in the flesh and then learn about its endangered status, its habitat and the zoo community's plans for its future, they are more likely to have empathy with both the species and the plans. Fuelled by this empathy, the public may be better informed, contribute financially to conservation causes and be better ambassadors for the interests of that species. This effect, it is argued, cannot be mimicked by wildlife films, books and education alone.

The second, and opposing, point of view is that because people can see the species in zoos and parks and because they are given information on how vulnerable the animal's habitat is and the fragility of its existence in the wild, they may receive the impression that there are plenty of a given species in captivity (surely a far better place for it anyway) and therefore not much reason to really worry about its future. If the visitor goes on to learn about species survival programmes, the success of captive breeding and how the only chance for that species is in captivity, then the tendency is for that visitor to leave the zoo feeling complacent and satisfied that endangered species are being protected and preserved and there is no real need for them to do any more. In the roadside zoos of Canada, for example, the most represented species of the large mammals is the cougar or mountain lion. The fact that this is a circulating population of captive animals does not detract from the impression given that this must be an animal well represented in the wild. In fact, in eastern Canada, the cougar is so rare it is almost never seen, and in western Canada is threatened in many areas.

In zoos, the public are being both reassured that the survival of a given species is in safe hands and that the fight for the habitat is as good as lost, as well as being secondary to the importance of the survival of the species itself. Article 2 of the Biodiversity Convention states that ex situ measures, including those in zoos, are "predominantly for the purpose of complementing in situ measures" and that conservation should be "preferably in the country of origin". Whilst *ex situ* measures have been important components in the preservation of a small number of species (e.g. golden lion tamarin, red wolf, Sumatran tiger, black-footed ferret, Arabian oryx) zoos tend to give the impression that they are pivotal in the conservation process. This tends to concentrate resources in zoos and diverts serious attention, resources and expertise from the in situ projects which are of paramount importance to long-term species survival and global conservation, because, after all, these species need to return to their habitat to halt the decline in biodiversity. Having them sitting around in zoos removes them as effectively from the environment as does extinction.

The complexities of international law and trade agreements, as discussed above, can also give a false sense of security to the public, who naturally wish to believe that the situation is improving. Moving species from one CITES category to another may appear insignificant on paper and may indeed be perceived as "good news", because the implication is that the population must be growing for trade and hunting restrictions to be relaxed. What is not understood is the political influence of countries that do not necessarily have the species' best interest at heart and who can sway decisions not necessarily based on scientific evidence that such a change in status is for the long term good of the species.

HOW IMPORTANT ARE ZOOS VERSUS IN SITU CONSERVATION?

The true role of zoos and wildlife parks in conservation is discussed in chapter 5 (by Rod Laidlaw): One of the most damning indictments of the role of zoos in reintroducing those species which they claim to be conserving was given in a recent paper by A. R. Glatson in the journal *Animal Welfare*. A footnote begins:

> Re-introduction is not specifically mentioned here as this is not generally a valid option.[14]

Yet, many people still believe that re-introduction (as distinct from restocking and rehabilitation) is the *raison d'être* of zoos and at some mythical future time all the animals at present in captivity – adapting slowly to the presence of man, eating prepared diets, leading largely slothful lives without the presence of predators or prey – will be released back into the wild to repopulate all those decimated regions and all will be well. It is a myth perpetuated by zoos, ignoring the flaws in the arguments which will be discussed elsewhere in this book.[15]

The most pressing reason for the public being aware of the merits of in situ conservation is Valmik Thapar's plea for the tiger:

> protecting the tiger in isolation is not the answer.[16]

It is not the answer for the tiger nor for us, nor for any other species, because, as David Hancocks[17] quotes from John Muir:

> When we try to pick out anything by itself, we find it hitched to everything else in the Universe.

What are the moral arguments involved in shaping human responses to endangered species?

Is conservation a science of value-free judgements; a means by which scientists, lawyers and conservationists measure, research, legislate for and record ways in which this planet, its environment, flora and fauna can adapt, develop and above all, survive that to which modern man is subjecting them? If it is value free, why are we bothering? Can conservation be without a moral dimension and exist as a concept? *The Oxford English Dictionary* defines conservation as:

> Preservation, esp of natural environment.

One of the definitions of preserve is "to keep safe". The idea of keeping something safe is immediately suggestive of protection, shelter, keeping free from harm, looking after; all terms associated with the powerful human need to nurture and cherish. Such a need could be argued to go beyond what is moral: we protect another human or an animal because we feel bound to by unconditional affection. One would never hear a mother describing looking after her children as a "moral duty", although society would regard it as such.

So perhaps conservation too goes beyond any moral obligation on our part. Society may regard it as our moral duty to protect our planet and the future of our children, but those involved in conservation would probably see their work more as a need: we are bound to preserve and protect the planet on which we live by the need to do more than just survive.

Endangered species cannot be separated from this argument since they are an integral part of conservation, but the issue of individual versus species does pose a different moral dilemma. Is the well-being of one individual or a small group of individuals of a species more important than the survival of that species as a whole? If by removing individuals from the wild (more common in the past, but still occurs) or sustaining a captive population, we are harming the physical or psychological welfare of those animals, can that harm be vindicated by citing conservation as the goal? The keeping of many individuals in captivity whose species are not threatened (but only might be at some time in the future) is more difficult to justify on moral grounds, but that is what zoos all over the world are doing in the name of keeping the turnstiles busy.

Some people argue that they and their children have a right to see such and such a species before it becomes extinct and that in itself is cause enough for keeping it in captivity. A proponent of such a cause may go so far as to say that society is morally obliged to provide the sight of these animals to those who can never afford to travel to see them. So, what if someone suddenly demanded that they would like to meet a Native American but could not afford to travel to do so? Should society "provide" by translocating a tribe or individual? (If this sounds ludicrous, remember that it was not so long ago that native peoples from all over the world were transported against their will to be "displayed" to the paying public.) The answer is, of course not; such a suggestion is morally wrong. It would also be misleading, for what the public would see is an individual from a different culture trying to adapt to their new situation. That is what we see when we view wild animals in captivity. And the moral argument is the same: we do not have the right to see these animals just because we would like to.

Does an individual animal have any concept of its "species"? Does it have any concept of preserving its species? Certainly animals recognize conspecifics; that is obvious and necessary from the point of view of reproduction, territorial behaviour, competition for resources and social behaviour. Reproduction is obviously an important biological function for which many animals will go to great lengths and risks to achieve successfully. Maternal/paternal protection of the young suggests that there is a need to preserve the life of offspring. But why? Is the need immediate, a response to a bond of affection or could animals have some perception of future generations? For that it would seem likely that they would need to share man's ego, and for that we have little evidence. If animals do not carry concepts of the future and of species survival then is the quality of individual life much more important to them than whether their kind lives on? And should human responses to endangered animals be directed to this consideration rather than preserving a species at all costs? Does the good of the many outweigh the good of the few? Such questions do not rest easily on the human conscience. Most of us would like to agree unconditionally with biologist Mark Carwardine's final statement in *Last Chance to See*[18] about the reason for caring about endangered species:

> it is simply this: the world would be a poorer, darker, lonelier place without them.

And at the same take John Webster's[19] words to heart when he talks about learning to understand domestic species in order to look after them and "control" their lives, in the sense of management; he highlights the difference between domestic and wild animals in the statement:

> since it is neither moral, nor practical, to control the life of a

> tiger, we should, if we understand them at all, learn to leave them alone.

Human responses to endangered species oscillate between the desire to control and the need to protect; understanding this may help us to achieve a balanced approach and prevent their suffocation by taking either tendency to its extreme.

Biodiversity is defined in Article 2 of The Biological Diversity Convention as:

> the variability among living organisms from all sources . . . including diversity within species, between species and ecosystems.

Notes

1. Convention on International Trade in endangered Species of Wild Fauna and Flora Treaty Series, no. 101, 1976.
2. Committee on the Status of Endangered Wildlife in Canada (COSEWIC), Definitions (as of 1990).
3. Convention on International Trade in endangered Species of Wild Fauna and Flora Treaty Series, no. 101, 1976.
4. D. Hancocks, *Adieu to the Zoo? Proceedings of Conservation and Animal Welfare – A New Era in Europe?* London School of Economics, 1995.
5. Ibid.
6. S. Lyster, *Conservation Treaties – Paper Tigers or Effective Conservation Tools? Proceedings of Conservation and Animal Welfare – A New Era in Europe?* London School of Economics, 1995.
7. Hancocks, *Adieu to the Zoo?*
8. D. Adams and M. Carwardine, *Last Chance to See*. London: Pan Books, 1991 (first published 1990, Heinemann).
9. V. Thapar, *The Tiger's Destiny*. London: Kyle Cathie Publishers, 1992.
10. Ibid.
11. Hancocks, *Adieu to the Zoo?*
12. Lyster, *Conservation Treaties*.
13. Ibid.
14. A. R. Glatson. "The control of zoo populations with specific reference to primates", *Animal Welfare*, vol. 7, pp. 269–81, 1998.
15. For a more detailed review of attitudes of the visiting public to zoos, see "Informal Learning at the Zoo: A Study of Attitude and Knowledge Impacts", 1989, a report by Dr Stephen Kellert (Yale University, School of Forestry and Environmental Studies, New Haven, CT) and Dr Julie Dunlap (Humane Society of the United States, Washington, D.C.) to the Zoological Society of Philadelphia, of a study funded by the G. R. Dodge Foundation.
16. Thapar, *The Tiger's Destiny*.
17. Hancocks, *Adieu to the Zoo?*
18. Adams and Carwardine, *Last Chance to See*.
19. A. J. F. Webster *Animal Welfare: A Cool Eye Towards Eden*. Oxford: Blackwell Science, 1994.

7 Traditional African beliefs

Credo Vusamazulu Mutwa

In old Africa people did not regard themselves as superior to the animals, the trees, and the fishes and the birds. They regarded themselves as part of all these living things and the weakest of all the creatures that God had created. This feeling of weakness instilled in their souls a deep dependence on the living nature around them.

Under western civilization we live in a world of separation in which things really are cruelly separated. There is confusion in the way we view the Earth and at the core of every great religion. God has been removed from the orbit of human life to some far away never-never land. We must take a great spiritual step backwards and adopt the views that were held by ancient Africans.

Through "Isilwane – The Animal", I hope to open the eyes of the world to traditional African attitudes, folklore and rituals which have governed the relationships between the people of Africa and the animal world.

Under western civilization, we live in a strange world of separatism; a world in which things that really belong together and which ought to be seen as part of a greater whole are cruelly separated. The result of this separatist attitude is that humanity is denied a great deal of valuable knowledge. We are led into a forest of confusion when we try to learn about ourselves, our mother, Planet Earth, and the universe of which our planet is an infinitesimal part.

Although there are many alternative attitudes it is very clear that during the last five hundred years or so the human race has made minimal, if any, progress in understanding itself, the world and the universe beyond. The much touted discoveries made by men such as Copernicus and Galileo, when viewed objectively, were really not discoveries at all, but rather rediscoveries of discoveries made hundreds, if not thousands, of years before.

People upon the plains and in the valleys of Africa knew, long before Galileo and Copernicus were born, that Planet Earth orbits the sun and not the other way round. Africans and people of other nations across the world knew thousands of years ago that Planet Earth was round; they knew that the world is but one of many worlds where living beings exist.

The Bushmen of the Kalahari Desert knew that no one could live on the moon, and that it lacked air and water. There is the legend of a stupid hunter who so feared living with other Bushmen that he decided to fly on magic wings to the moon. There he died of thirst and hunger because there was neither water nor animals upon that bleak satellite.

Today we see the human race running around in circles, like a mad dog chasing its own tail. We have seen things hailed as great discoveries which will change the future of humanity, end in cul-de-sacs of futility. Today, the same type of confusion prevails in all fields of human thought.

There is confusion in the way we view ourselves, there is confusion in the way we view Planet Earth, there is even confusion, believe it or not, at the core of every one of the world's great religions. I can state this with confidence, as I have studied most of these religions and even joined some of them.

But why the confusion? It is due to the way we view things: the way we view the atom, the stars, life on Planet Earth, and the way we view the Deity Himself or Herself. But the most dangerous and destructive view by far – one which has changed human beings into rampaging, destructive and mindless beasts – is that we compare ourselves with other living things.

Western man is taught that he is the master of all living things. The Bible itself enshrines this extreme attitude, as do other great books. Repeatedly one hears of western people talking about nature as if it were man's mortal enemy: one hears dangerous phrases such as "untamed nature" or "interrogating nature with power". One hears of the strange belief that man is superior to all other living things on Planet Earth, and that he was especially created to be overlord and custodian of all things, animate or inanimate.

Until these attitudes are combated and erased from the human mind, westernized human beings will be a danger to all earthly life, including themselves.

We are conditioned to regard nature as crude and primitive, to regard all stretches of forest, bush or savannah, as things that ought to be cleared before the so-called master of all, the human being, can rule supreme over the denuded valleys and the ravaged plains.

A very dangerous attitude that ought to be erased from our minds and those of our children is that human beings can build a glittering technological future without animals, and without trees; a future in which food will be synthesized (only heaven knows what from), in which there will be no disease and no death. This Utopian attitude encourages human beings to ravage the Planet Earth in the hope that our descendants, who will inherit our denuded world, will somehow, using the might of the electron and waving the magic wand of technology, create a new paradise.

One thing that I, as a traditional African, angrily frown upon is that, in western civilization, God is removed from the orbit of human life to some faraway, never-never heaven. Expelling God from everyday life leaves the field clear for super-capitalists, colonialists and other plunderers to rape the Planet Earth, to destroy nature, to ravage priceless natural resources with cold impunity.

African people have the amusing saying that once a tribe has sent its chief into exile, slaughtered its elders and traditional healers, and kicked out its warriors and praise-singers, it turns into a nation of long-fanged, man-eating cannibals. Throughout the world this is what human beings have become: big-bellied, insatiable, unbelievably greedy cannibals.

We have become a nation like the legendary monkeys who, according to one African story, were placed by the great Earth Mother on a sacred fig tree to guard it. They developed such appetites that they not only ate all the figs but also devoured the bark and the wood of the tree. When the great Earth Mother returned, she found the tree reduced to a rotting stump and the skeletons of all the monkeys who had died of starvation after eating their own tree.

How can we escape from the ugly trap in which our own shortsightedness, greed and gross stupidity have landed us? How can we get out of this prison?

We must take a great spiritual step backwards. We must adopt the view of creation that was held not only by ancient Africans, but also by native Americans and many other people of the ancient world: that creation is one great and beautiful whole, one revolving sphere of the purest, greenest crystal, a sphere to be viewed from all sides as one thing, instead of a number of shattered fragments upon the dark desert of human folly.

We must stop – immediately – regarding ourselves as superior and special creatures created in the image of some imaginary god. This dangerous, chauvinistic view has led us to the very edge of destruction. We must bring the Almighty back into our lives – not just on Sunday or Saturday, but every hour and day.

And, as strange as this may sound to those who believe in it, we must stop believing that man's ultimate destiny is in some heaven beyond the dark curtain of death.

In olden days people viewed heaven and Earth, the spiritual and the physical, as one beautiful thing. People viewed God as being not only with us on Earth and in heaven, but also within us. We were taught by ancient Africans that we are part of God (as a little pebble is part of a great mountain), and because of this, we should beware of doing anything against the teaching and the nature of God.

In old Africa we did not regard ourselves as superior to the animals, the trees, and the fishes and the birds. We regarded ourselves as part of all these living things. We believed that far from being specially created, we were, in fact, the weakest of all the creatures that God created. This feeling of weakness instilled in our souls a deep dependence upon the living nature around us.

We believed that human beings could not exist without animals, birds and fishes, or the greenery that whispers all around us. We used to believe that in every one of us there lay a spiritual animal, bird and fish with which we should keep contact at all times, to anchor our family upon the shifting surface of this often troubled planet.

We believed that within us were the oceans, the rivers, the sky and the mountains. We believed that we had nature within and beyond ourselves. For this reason, many African gods were depicted as part animal and part human. For instance, the great Earth Mother, whose Zulu name is Nomkhubulwane, or simply "Ma" is often depicted with only one human leg, while her other leg is that of an animal – an antelope, elephant or rhinoceros. At other times she is depicted as having one fully human leg and another, usually the left leg, with roots where one would expect to find toes.

The great Earth Mother, together with other lesser goddesses, was believed by African people to be capable of changing her shape to that of any animal, bird or fish whenever she chose, and this is why Zulus call her Nomkhubulwane, a name which means "she who chooses the state of an animal" – in short, "the shape-changer".

Nomkhubulane is a goddess believed to be a trinity within herself. She is thought to consist of a young woman whose name is Nomndende, which means "lady of the big buttocks" or "lady of the big hips"; a middle-aged woman, called Nomkhubulwane, and, as her bad aspect, Nomhoyi, a hideous, ugly, wrinkled old hag, with fangs like a shark's.

The great Earth Mother is capable of changing her shape into beautiful and gentle birds, animals and reptiles. She is capable of assuming the shape of an animal such as a springbok, an eland, an impala, a lizard, or a python. She is believed to be able to change her shape into a rhinoceros, an elephant, a giraffe, a lion or a lioness at will.

But in her bad and cruel aspect, she is believed to be capable of changing her shape into only two animals: the hyena or the crocodile. Some say that she likes to change into a vulture. This is the most popular belief about this most ancient of African goddesses.

Initiation schools still exist in scattered parts of Africa, where one learns about the deepest spiritual mysteries of our people and our country. We are taught that the reason that our forefathers told us that our gods and goddesses were capable of changing shape, or were part animal and part human beings, is that they wanted to instill in the midst of their descendants the oneness of the human being, the animal and the Deity.

By making us believe that the highest gods were part animal and part human being, we were taught to look upon animals with great reverence, love and respect. If you are taught that God often has the head of a lion and the body of a human being, you will treat all lions with respect.

In my travels to many parts of the world and in the course of my studies of ancient history and religions, I have noticed with interest that all the nations which treated nature with great respect, recognized people's dependence on her bounty as human beings, created civilizations in which nature was worshipped as a Deity, and did not separate nature from human life had, among their gods and goddesses, beings who were part animal and part human being.

The ancient Egyptians who depended upon the Nile had many such gods. The ancient Sumerians, too, had in their pantheons gods who were part animal and part human being. The God Ningishieda was depicted as being part bull and part human being.

I have also noticed that all the native races of America – South, Central and North – had gods exactly like this. In the United States, for example, I found the Hopi people believing in, among many other spiritual beings, a female being which they call Hanu-Manu. Hanu-Manu, the goddess of maize and greenery, is depicted as a beautiful American-Indian woman with bright green skin and long, black hair.

African people depict Nomkhubulwane in exactly the same way – as a green or silver skinned goddess with long, black hair. The Egyptian God of fertility Ozaries or Asaar, is also depicted as having green skin. It is interesting to note that, among the Zulu people, when a person is born with a particularly dark skin, he or she is not called black-skinned, but green-skinned. The Zulu word for black is mnyama. This term is never used to address a dark-skinned person to whom we wish to show respect. We rather use the term luhlaza, which means "green" or "green-skinned".

In ancient times, all the men and women who trained as traditional healers or sangomas and who had particularly dark skins were specially selected to learn about plants and animals, and ways of combating disease in both of these life forms. At one time, my grandfather toyed with the idea of training me as a healer of domestic animals because of my dark skin.

"Isilwane – The Animal" will reveal African attitudes to animals: domestic, wild, on land, in the sea and in rivers.

When you talk of wildlife conservation nowadays, many people assume you are talking about something new, a miracle born of our supposedly enlightened era, a sign that human beings are beginning to care about the world in which they live, and about animals and other forms of life. But wildlife conservation is as old as Africa.

When white people came to this land, they found the plains and the valleys of the so-called Dark Continent teeming with wildlife. From the Cape to Central Africa and beyond, the land was alive with millions of animals. Great herds used to migrate the length and breadth of Africa. Millions of springbok, wildebeest, zebra and buffalo swarmed across the land, like bees around a beehive.

What many people do not realize is that these huge, wild herds existed because the native people of Africa regarded them as a blessing from the gods, as something unbelievably sacred and vital for the continued existence of human beings. Black people believed that animals were the blood of the Earth and that as long as there were migrations criss-crossing the country, human existence on Earth was guaranteed.

No one ever interfered with these great migrations because they really believed that wildlife was the soul, the very life-blood, of Mother Earth.

When white people came to Africa, they had been conditioned to separate themselves spiritually and physically from wildlife. In the vast herds of animals they saw four-footed enemies to be crushed and objects of fun to be destroyed for pleasure. They slaughtered wild animals by the million.

It never occurred to white pioneers that these animals were protected by the native tribes through whose land they migrated. It never occurred to them, with their muskets, rifles and carbines, that black people worshipped these great herds and regarded them as an integral part of their existence on Earth.

Many hundreds of years ago, a wise old man called Pinda Moleli prophesied that one of the first indications that the end of the world had come would be the disappearance of herds from the African plains. The herds have almost disappeared and Pinda Moleli's prophesy appears to be coming true.

In old Africa, every tribe had an animal that it regarded as its totem, an animal after which the tribe had been named by its founders. It was the sacred duty of this tribe to ensure that the animal after which it was named was never harmed within the confines of its territory.

In addition, Africans knew that certain wild animals co-exist with others, and that in order to protect the animal after which the tribe was named, it was essential to protect those animals with which the sacred one co-existed.

In KwaZulu-Natal, for example, there is a tribe, the Dube people, for whom the zebra is the totem. These people not only protect vast herds of zebra in their tribal land, allowing them to roam wherever they choose, but they also protect herds of wildebeest because they realize that zebras co-exist with wildebeest.

The zebra has very good eyesight during the day but very poor eyesight at night. The opposite is true for the wildebeest. And so these two very dissimilar animals are always found grazing together in the bush for mutual protection. The old Africans knew that to protect the zebra effectively one had to protect the wildebeest, the warthog, the bushpig, the eland, the kudu and other animals sometimes found grazing with zebra in the bush.

But the old Africans knew that it was not enough simply to protect those animals which grazed with their tribal totem. It was essential to protect those animals which preyed upon the sacred animals.

Thus, those who protect the zebra and all other grass-eating animals that graze with it must also protect the preying lion. People knew that although the lion was the zebra's enemy, it was a natural and necessary enemy that would weed out the weaker zebra and ensure the survival of the fittest.

There were other tribes, such as the Botswana Bakaru and the Bafarutsi, which regarded the baboon as their totem. They knew that protecting baboons alone was not enough. The leopard which preyed upon baboons had to be protected, along with those plants upon which the baboons fed. The people knew that if they did not protect these plants, they would starve in the bush and start feeding on the crops in the people's corn and maize fields. If this occurred, baboons would become man's enemy.

The Botswana Batloung tribe, whose name means "people of the elephant", were sworn to protect the elephant. They also protected the rhinoceros and the hippopotamus, which they regarded as the elephant's cousins. It was believed that an elephant would not injure a person who carried the Bafloung name.

But what if an elephant became a rogue and started devastating villages? What if an elephant became a destroyer and started terrorising the people? If this occurred, the tribe's king would call a gathering of his wisest people, among whom would be the traditional healers. They would throw the bones of divination and seek the answers from spirits as to exactly why the elephant had become an enemy.

If the diviners found that the elephant was sick or had been harassed by human beings in any way, strenuous efforts – some of them quite dangerous and bizarre – were made to entice the rogue elephant away from Bafloung territory without it being killed. However, should it prove absolutely necessary to kill the elephant, a group of hunters who were not of the Bafloung nation had to be brought in from far away.

The hunters would kill the elephant and then flee as fast as they could, back to their native land, for if they were caught having killed an elephant in Bafloung territory, they too stood a chance of being killed. A reward in the form of cattle would be sent by the Bafloung to the hunters for their troubles.

If one of the hunters was killed during the elephant hunt, as often happened, he would be given a hero's burial by the Bafloung. He would be regarded as one of the Bafloung nation and be honoured in spirit by the people he had helped.

One of the most important pillars upon which the traditional religion of African people rests is a belief in reincarnation and the transmigration of souls. There is the belief that when you die, you are reincarnated immediately after death as that type of animal which your people regard as their totem.

The Zulu people had twelve totems, among which were the elephant, the lion, the leopard and the fierce snake that is known as the mamba. Zulu people believed that when one of their kings died, he would be reincarnated as a mamba. If, after the death of a king, a mamba was seen entering the king's kraal, this was taken as a sign that the king had returned to his people, inside the body of the mamba. While the mamba was in the hut, that hut and several others next to it would be evacuated of all human life. The mamba was allowed to stay in peace inside the hut for as long as it chose.

Zulu people never willingly killed a lion, as it was the symbol of their king and his surrogate. In old Zululand, any stranger who killed a lion lived to regret it!

There were tribes who had certain birds as their totem and who protected them with their lives, if necessary. Some tribes who had particular trees as their totem also guarded these with their lives.

Among the Botswana and the Basotho people there was a very ancient tribe called the Mgwana, "the crocodile people", who regarded the crocodile as their totem and their holiest animal symbol. If a Mgwani was killed by an elephant, he was deeply mourned, but if a Mgwani was killed by a crocodile, it was believed either that he had been greatly honoured by one of his ancestral spirits or that he had angered them.

In the land once called Rhodesia and now known as Zimbabwe, there is a tribe of people who also regard the crocodile as their totem. These people are the Tangwane people, a name which also means "people of the crocodile".

The Tangwane people were deeply humiliated by a group of white colonialists, among whom was a particular gentleman from England who held black people in utter contempt. The white officers and other officials caused great suffering to a very holy chief, called Rekhi Tangwane, whom they had treated cruelly and with disrespect. One day, in my presence, a group of Tangwane elders met under a tree and solemnly placed a curse on the worst of the white officials. They prayed to the great crocodile of heaven to bring immediate death to the white man who had insulted and injured their chief. They made an image of this man from clay and then they shattered it ceremonially with a crocodile carved out of Rhodesian teak.

A few weeks later, a vehicle in which the official was travelling stalled while crossing a river. The official was seized and savagely mauled by a crocodile which appeared from nowhere. Someone managed to shoot the crocodile and save him, but he later died from the severe injuries. Needless to say the Tangwane people believed that one of their ancestral spirits had been sent to punish the man, and his lingering painful death was regarded as quite befitting the crime committed against their holy chief.

The lives of ordinary human beings are full of coincidences and so is history. Today, there are many South African game reserves set aside to protect wild animals. What is amazing to a student of tribal history is that many of these game reserves were established by white operatives in areas which had already been claimed as lands of animals by some of our greatest kings, hundreds of years ago. For example, everyone knows about South Africa's Kruger National Park, but very few realize that it was a sacred land of animals where great Shangani kings forbade all hunting without royal permission.

In KwaZulu-Natal, the Umfolozi Game Reserve and the Ndumo Game Reserve were first proclaimed by Shaka as far back as 1823, when that great and far sighted, though fiercely warlike, Zulu monarch set aside areas where animals were to exist without interference by human beings. A game reserve was not just a place where animals dwelt in peace, it was set aside with gods and animals in mind. A game reserve was regarded as the sacred place of the gods where no hunting or shedding of blood was allowed. In the Umfolozi area, only the king was allowed to hunt animals, and then only on very sacred occasions.

Africans did not hunt animals for fun. They were hunted for food and for religious reasons. In many instances a religious hunt was conducted by the king once, and once only, during his lifetime.

In the land now called Botswana there exists a very spiritual place which, these days, is called the Tuli Block. The great King Khama, who ruled the country during the 19th century, forbade all hunting for a very strange reason. It is said that King Khama and his men were hunting in the Tuli Block near the Shashi River, one of the holiest rivers in southern Africa, when they suddenly saw, descending from the heavens, a great glowing sphere of light. The light hovered above the ground for a long time and was seen by more than a hundred armed warriors. It is said that, clearly visible inside this glowing sphere of light, there were two gigantic, man-like entities which stood facing each other and performing mysterious tasks with their hands.

After this incident, King Khama declared the entire Tuli Block a sacred place where all hunting and shedding of blood was forbidden for all time.

If you want to learn about the true greatness of the black people of Africa, you must examine the hundreds of wise sayings of every tribe and nation. Here, you will discover the depth of African traditional wisdom and knowledge. If you study these proverbs you will find, for example, that Africans knew about the importance of a healthy, clean environment long before other people.

The African people knew, just as the native American people knew, that if you destroy the environment, you will ultimately destroy the human race. Among many African proverbs to do with the environment and with animals is this one: "That which scratches the wild animal, also scratches the human being." This proverb means that if you do evil to wild animals, evil will ultimately rebound on your fellow human beings.

A remarkable Tswana proverb states that "He who buries the tree will next bury the wild animal, and after that, bury his own ox, and ultimately, bury his own children." This saying indicates that people were aware, even in ancient times, of the interdependence of all living creatures upon this Earth, and that if you harm one, you harm others and, in the end, yourself.

Although African people kept livestock in the form of cattle, sheep, goats and chickens, they were sometimes forced by necessity to go into the wilds in search of animals whose skins could be used for blankets, bags, and items of attire. These animals were very often dassies (also called rock rabbits or hyraxes) or black-backed jackals, and from time to time, large antelopes.

The hunt was always governed by very strict rules and taboos. Elders kept a close watch on all the hunters to make sure that no-one brought down more animals than was necessary for meat and for skins. You were not allowed to hunt more animals than you actually needed, and you were not allowed to leave the carcass rotting in the bush. This was regarded as very unlucky.

In other words, you were not allowed to bring back more than you could carry or more than your family could use within a given time.

Hunting was always preceded and followed by elaborate rituals: a knot was tied in the tail-hairs of the animal which had been brought down, as a gesture to the souls of the dead animal requesting it to forgive the hunters for robbing it of its living home and wishing it a speedy rebirth.

Africans carefully studied the animals' way of life and all hunting was forbidden when it was mating season and when animals were pregnant with young. It was regarded as the blackest of bad luck for a hunter to bring down a pregnant antelope. If this happened, it was believed that one of the hunter's wives would die during childbirth.

Although Africans had domesticated animals such as dogs and cats, they often enlisted the assistance of wild animals under certain circumstances in their daily lives. For example, all large African villages produced piles of bones from the meat eaten by the villagers, especially military kraals which housed as many as ten thousand warriors. These warriors were great meat-eaters and piles of bones accumulated outside the stockade of each kraal.

The warriors encouraged large groups of hyena to live in the bush, as these scavengers disposed of the bones. The warriors and their families also encouraged warthogs and bushpigs to live peacefully outside the kraal – and sometimes inside the kraal. The role of these greedy animals was to dispose of left-over food scraps in the form of corncakes and stale maize porridge.

African kings rejoiced every time migrating animals thundered through their kingdoms, for they knew that these animals would leave a great swathe of dung along the route. When the rains came, the bush would be green and the grass would grow tall as a result of the fertilization of the land by the herds.

It is a fact well known to all students of Zulu history that the vulture enjoyed special favour in the eyes of Zulu kings, as did hyena and jackal. These birds, which were known as izinyoni-ze-nkosi, or "the birds of the king", helped to dispose of the corpses of executed criminals which were dumped in deep gullies not far from the kings' great kraals.

Criminals were not given the honour of a decent burial under Zulu culture, but were thrown into a gully after execution for vultures to feast upon. Even today, the Zulus have a saying, "You shall die and be eaten by vultures," which refers to a person who will be punished for committing a heinous crime.

Africans occasionally captured living wild animals to extract what they regarded as medicinal substances. For example, they knew that the eland produced much richer milk than a domestic cow and that it had powerful medicinal properties for helping children. When a Zulu child was weak and sickly at birth, the child was often fed eland's milk. The eland cows were specially captured and milked for this purpose before being released and sent scampering back into the bush. Zulus sometimes captured living hyena, plucked hairs off their tails and then released them back into the wild. They believed that the tail-hairs of a hyena, and even its whiskers, could induce sleep in sleepless children if the hairs were burnt on charcoal.

It is a known fact that African warriors wore head-dresses made from, among other things, the feathers of birds such as ostriches, herons and eagles. However, many people do not know that a warrior never wore the feathers of a bird that he had killed, as this was regarded as very unlucky. The bird had to be alive when the feathers were taken from its wing or tail, then be released. Great care was taken to remove only those feathers which would in no way impair the bird's flight or wellbeing.

When I was a young boy, my grandfather taught me how to capture a bird and remove two of its feathers. A hole was dug that was big enough for me to stand upright in, a lid of saplings and green branches was laid over the hole and a young dassie or hare was tied to the top. When a bird, such as a large eagle, soared down to snatch the animal, the boy hidden under the lid would reach out and pluck two feathers from the tail or the wings as it struggled to lift its prey. It was a risky task which, if one was careless, would result in badly lacerated arms. If you did it carefully, though, you were rewarded with two feathers from a live eagle which would then soar heavenwards, carrying its prey with it, and you would earn the praise of your elders and peers for your great cunning and courage.

The everyday life of the African of old was governed by scores of taboos, many of which related to the protection of nature, the environment and wildlife, and the protection of domestic animals against acts of cruelty by human beings.

Certain trees were not allowed to be cut down for any reason whatsoever, and there were others which could be cut down only on very special occasion or for very serious reasons.

Among the Botswana people, for example, there is a type of

acacia tree known as the moosu tree which is only cut down when a local chief dies. It is used to make firewood for the ritual fire that is lit outside the king's home, to light the king's soul to the next world. No-one, even today, is allowed to cut down a moosu tree. If you do, the Botswana will publicly accuse you of wishing for the death of their king and you will be severely punished for this crime.

The umphafa tree grows in KwaZulu-Natal and other parts of South Africa. No-one was allowed to cut a branch from this tree without first obtaining the permission of the chief or king. In olden days, this tree was used to make cattle pens because the wood is never eaten by termites and it can last for years. Even if the king had given his permission, you were only allowed to cut off old branches. Cutting off new branches was strictly forbidden, and no more than two branches could be removed from each large tree.

Traditional healers used the bark of different trees in their battle against disease, but when a traditional healer went into the bush to source medicinal bark or roots, he or she was not allowed to take so much bark that if the tree from which he or she obtained the bark was destroyed, all the patients treated with the bark from that tree would die.

So it was in the interests of the traditional healer to keep the tree from which he or she had taken medicinal bark alive and well. No ring-barking was allowed, and only bark from very old branches could be taken.

If modern poachers and defilers of the environment think that game reserve wardens and environment protection officers inflict harsh punishments upon them, they should actually breathe a sigh of relief. In old Africa, if you were caught polluting the environment in any way, no fine or apology was acceptable. Death, and only death – often the most cruel imaginable – was the punishment.

The story is told of a young man who lived in the days of the great King Jobe of the Mthethwa people. He had the strange and offensive habit of urinating into any river or stream he came across. One day, King Jobe was told of this, and decided to make an example of the offender.

The young man was seen urinating into a spring and was promptly arrested by warriors and brought before King Jobe. With a cruel smile upon his face, King Jobe ordered that the young man drink huge volumes of marula beer, which is a very diuretic liquid. Then the young man was fed a huge meal of corncakes and fat goat's meat.

Then the king ordered that a piece of raw hide be tied around the young man's penis so that he was unable to urinate, and a large mealie cob forced into his anus to prevent him from defecating. The helpless young man was then buried up to his waist in a hole in the ground to ensure that he was incapable of relieving himself. He suffered horribly for several days before the king dispatched him with a savage battle-axe blow to the head.

In old KwaZulu-Natal and in other parts of the country, the ancient laws of protecting Mother Earth were enforced to the letter.

If a person was caught throwing refuse or a dead animal into a river or stream, or caught cutting down a tree which the law forbade, then that person was tied hand and foot, his or her belly was slashed open, and the intestines pulled out and tied around the branches of a thorn tree. The victim was left to die a horrible death. Sometimes the victim's eyes and lips were stitched closed with sinew and then he or she was forced to walk through bush where there were man-eating animals.

If you were responsible for killing a sacred animal, you were first beaten unconscious by a troop of women and then, if you were male, you were publicly castrated or, if you were female, your breasts were slashed off. It was said that the great Earth Mother is a very sensitive and quick-tempered goddess, and that only the hideous death of those who offend her can placate her and prevent her from taking revenge on the rest of the tribe.

The short-sighted, arrogant and mindless modern savages who pollute our rivers with industrial effluent and defile the skies with acid rain, and the skulking poachers who murder rhinoceros throughout the continent of Africa today, really ought to consider themselves lucky that they were not born a century or more ago. Had they done what they are doing today in the days of King Jobe, they would have had many hours of regret before the dark angel of death came to relieve them from their agony.

It is not an exaggeration to say that African people had more laws governing people's behaviour towards the Earth, plants and animals than they had governing other acts of human behaviour. When crops were planted, we conducted rituals not only with the aim of ensuring a good harvest, but also to thank the Earth Mother and to apologize for injuring her sacred flesh in order to plant food.

When we hoed to get rid of weeds, rituals were performed as a form of apology to the weeds for having to remove them to save our crops. We understood that weeds were not evil, but were plants which had the misfortune of growing where we had planted our food crops.

At harvest time, we left some of our corn standing so that passing birds could share in the bounty of our fields and, by sharing, bless us and ensure us of plenty of food. Sometimes large fields of corn and millet were planted. These were sacred to the goddess and were offered to the vast armies of birds to eat. No human being could enter the sacred cornfield.

These sacred fields were ploughed far from the ordinary millet, maize and corn, and they were left unfenced. Over the centuries, people had discovered that the star gods sometimes communicated with human beings through these sacred fields. Time and again, strange circular depressions were seen in the centre of these fields.

These depressions were called izishoze zamatongo, the great circles of the gods.

These circles are an amazing sight to see. The stalks of corn or millet are never cut by the gods when they form these depressions. It appears as though a great, circular, disk-shaped force has descended on the field. It presses the corn firmly into the ground, without breaking the stalks or damaging the plants. Then the force appears to spin, resulting in the strange spiral appearance of the fallen stalks. Words cannot describe such a phenomenon, which I have seen more than thirty times in the course of my life as a traditional healer. Whenever a circle appeared in the fields, the people rushed to erect a fence of poles around the circle. They would dance and perform other sacred rituals honouring the star gods and the Earth Mother.

All the kings and chiefs awaited the arrival of these circles. The appearance would be cause for celebrations which lasted several days. These celebrations were accompanied by prayers to the gods to watch over the people and to talk to them through the sacred circles.

When Africans ploughed the sacred and the ordinary grain fields, they never raked out the stumps of the previous year's corn. They were ploughed under to feed the soil and keep it fertile.

Many tribes practised a strange ritual, especially during winter, when they gathered all the left-overs from their meals in grass baskets every two or three days and took them to the cornfields where they were ceremonially buried. This was done while the fields were fallow and was called "feeding the grandmother". This ritual, which our grandparents told us was thousands of years old, was practised as recently as my childhood years, until it was forbidden by over-zealous and ignorant missionaries.

In olden times, African tribes were forced by law to recycle the ash from cooking fires. If the village's ash dump showed signs of growing too big, some of the ash was taken away in baskets, mixed with sand and water to form a cement-like paste, and used to repair hut floors. It was also used to build paths in front of huts and the low mud walls that bordered these places.

Ash was also made into a paint and used to rid cattle of ticks. If a cow was heavily infested with ticks, you dug a hole, filled it with ash and water, mixed it into paint similar to whitewash and then, using a broom, painted the cow with it. Ticks would drop off the beast and it would be relieved of its agony.

Some tribes, such as the Botswana, had another ingenious way of ridding cattle of ticks using wood ash. They would dig a hole just outside the entrance to their cattle-pens and fill it with ash. When the cattle were driven in and out of the pen, they passed through this heap of ash, and this caused the ticks to drop off.

Ash was also used as a disinfectant. If anyone died of an infectious disease, they were buried in an ash dump. Very deep graves were dug and some ash was poured into it before the person was buried. When the grave had been filled, a heap of ash was poured over it to prevent the disease from killing others. Africans believed that negative spirits were afraid of wood ash, and it was used freely in combating these entities.

Some people believed that ticks were the offspring of evil spirits as they could not stand being covered with ash.

One of the laws protecting the environment was that high-ranking people were strictly forbidden from eating particular types of food. It was believed that certain foods, which were freely eaten by ordinary people, would cause droughts and other ecological disasters if consumed by high-ranking people.

For example, there is a very nutritious bean which the Zulus call indumba (cowpea), which is particularly delicious when boiled in water with a little cow fat and salt. Traditional healers and clairvoyants are forbidden from eating indumba. It is said that if a sangome or an inyanga eats these beans, all the good spirits will take flight and ill-luck in the form of cattle disease or man-killing epidemics will call upon the community.

There is also a kind of sweet cane, called imfe, which many Zulus love to chew when it is in season. Delicious as it is to eat, and beneficial though it is because of its fibre content and tooth-cleaning properties, imfe is forbidden to chiefs, princes and princesses. It is said that if a person of royal blood breaks the taboo and chews imfe, and great illness will affect cattle and human beings, and crops will perish in a great drought.

One day, King Langalibalele, who lived in the Natal Midlands during the 19th century, yielded to temptation and chewed some imfe. A great blight ruined his people's cornfields and a savage disease that had never been seen before in that area swept away hundreds of cattle. To this day, traditional historians always point out Langalibile's mistake. He is called the king who chewed imfe and caused the death of his country.

Before I end this chapter [which forms the introduction to the author's book *Isilwane – The Animal*], let me tell you about two more taboos, the breaking of which is said to bring great disaster to the offender's land.

Many years ago, when I was still a child, one of my father's half-brothers kicked down the door of his rondavel and caught his wife and a neighbour in bed together. My father's half-brother took his knobkerrie and beat the man to within an inch of his adulterous life. And then he took a sjambok and beat his wife. The matter was brought before the tribal court in the chief's village and my father's half-brother was fined five head of cattle because he had broken the taboo that forbade wife-beating. It was believed that if a man thrashed his spouse during the growing season, the great mother goddess and the female ancestral spirits would withhold rain from the country as punishment for this offence.

While corn, maize, millet and pumpkins were growing in the fields, no one was allowed to beat any female for any reason, even if she had committed a crime.

Herd-boys carried long whips with which they controlled cattle while they drove them between the pastures and the cattle-pens. During the growing season, you were not allowed to use your whip on cows, nanny-goats and ewes. You could crack the whip to frighten a cow into returning to the herd if she showed signs of wandering, but you were not allowed to whip her. African laws and taboos were sometimes very strange indeed.

One of the holiest substances known to Africans is salt. Salt is regarded as the sweat of the great Earth Mother, crystallized by the sun God for the benefit of human beings and animals. For many centuries, Africans treated salt with respect, and in many urban and rural areas of South Africa this is still the case. The ancient laws of Africa die hard.

I wish you happy reading, enlightenment and peace.

8 From Conservation to Coexistence

Gareth Patterson

This chapter deals with the need to transform present-day "Conservation" – the use of natural resources for the benefit of humankind – into a holistic approach of preserving nature for its own intrinsic value and for its spiritual value to humankind. The chapter also deals with the urgent need for humankind to begin to re-identify with all life, to feel a part of all life and not apart from all life.

Conservation means different things to different people and therein lies many dangers. To some it means protection, that is to say preservation of wildlife and wilderness purely for its own intrinsic value.

To others, such as South African conservationists it means sustainable use, or "Wise Use" as they want to call it, of natural resources for the maximum benefit of humankind.

Some conservationists use the term in a way that is passive or benign. I believe it is another word for management, for this day and age the prevailing philosophy is "its got to pay to stay". Conservation in its many guises has also been a political tool in southern Africa.

For example, from the 1920s onwards, "conservation" in South Africa became a political white nationalist symbol. The Kruger National Park was named as such for politically loaded reasons. In the 1920s, minister of Lands, in South Africa, P. G. W. Grobler, declared that "it is due to the farsightedness of the late president Kruger that we are today able to establish a park". In reality, that "farsightedness" of the late president Kruger in fact never existed. It has recently been revealed that "never in his (Kruger) life thought of wildlife except as biltong (dried meat) . . . " And that "I wonder, I repeat what he (Kruger) could say could he see himself depicted as the 'saviour of the South African game'!!" so wrote Kruger National Park warden Stevenson Hamilton in a private letter in the 1920s.

Conservation in the Kruger National Park became different things to different people. Foreign tourists perceived the National Park as a showcase of southern African wildlife. The middle class white South Africans saw it as a place of recreation and a romanticized reminder of "how things once were". And the black people? The views of the many who had been evicted from their ancestral land to live outside the park in 'tribal reserves', and denied access to wildlife as a traditional component of subsistence? Theirs was a view that conservation and game reserves were white man's concepts and inventions, which put wildlife above black people and were instruments of dispossession and subjugation.

Of this, Jane Carruthers wrote in her book *The Kruger National Park – A Social and Political History*:

> The National Park ideology . . . reinvigorated the exclusion of Africans and consolidated the process of co-opting wildlife conservation into the orbit of white culture and that, within decades, the National Park was being overtly exploited to exemplify and inculcate South African culture, including casting Africans homogeneously in the role of poachers and whites in the role of conservationists.

To the true Africans, conservation was viewed as a further tool of subjugation deriving from the whites' separatist doctrines. Unlike the western beliefs of being the master of living things and of human supremacy over nature, traditional African pantheistic beliefs have no sharp distinctions between God and nature, no exact boundary between man's habitat and that of wild animals, and believed that God was present in everything – the animate and the inanimate. Of this, the African sage Credo Mutwa wrote in his book *Isilwane – The Animal*:

> We were taught by ancient Africans that we are part of God (as a little pebble is part of a great mountain) and because of this, we should beware of doing anything against the teaching and the nature of God. In old Africa we did not regard ourselves as superiors to the animals, the trees and the fishes and the birds. We regarded ourselves as part of all these living things.

Credo also wrote that:

> We believed that human beings could not exist without the animals, birds and fishes or the greenery that whispers all around us . . . we believed that we had nature within and beyond ourselves . . .

The African worldview was a totally inclusive one, one of being a part of the overall whole. Today, I believe we must look again and listen and hopefully learn from the enviro-religious experience of the traditional African people. Perhaps, in turn, western people can recapture some of the solidarity, the serenity and the healing which is so needed to nurture ourselves spiritually and to heal the injuries inflicted on nature in Africa.

Conservation needs to be transformed by the rediscovery of the African art of coexistence. To do this, we need to see wildlife, the wild places, other people and ourselves as being a part of nature. Feeling a part of all things natural is spiritually liberating. By so doing, one is freed from loneliness of spirit. Naturally, once you do, you are no longer alone. And by being a part of the whole, of God, man's solidarity with nature and God is achieved. This is the foundation of the art of coexistence.

Western attitudes and beliefs gave birth to the inventions of "Game Reserves" and "Tribal Reserves" – which in turn effectively separated two parts of a natural and life affirming whole. The ramifications of this separation have been damaging. It has led to the belief that nature is harmonious only when man is absent from nature (i.e. game reserves, national parks etc). This has led to the perception that the animals are nicely protected in nature in reserves – but also that there is not much hope (or place) for wildlife outside the game reserves and national parks. As conservationist David Western wrote in his book *In the Dust of Kilimanjaro*: by becoming separated from nature, respect, knowledge and caring for the land has died in the hearts of modern man. He goes on to say that man's view has become a limited one and his connection with nature has been replaced with materialism and technology. But of course man is nature, and nature is man, otherwise man becomes unnatural, and unnaturally he will seal his own fate – and that of nature.

We must now again embrace an inclusive worldview, and rediscover the art of coexistence. With coexistence, there is automatically more space available for wildlife. In turn, the prospects for conservation (which can then be read as coexistence) would become limitless.

The following poem sums up what I am trying to relate.

The Earth deserves our love
Only the unnaturals
Can live so at ease
While they poison the lands
Rape her for profit
Bleed her for oil
And not even attempt
To heal the wounds . . .

Only the unnaturals
Rule our lands today
So deaf to the wailing
Of our skies, of our hungry,
Of the strange new disease
And of that dying earth
Bleeding and wounded

And breeding only deserts
Where once there were
The proud trees of Africa . . .

And we live in unnatural times
And we must make it
Natural again
With our singing
And our intelligent rage
Ben Okri – For Ken Saro-wiwa

The CON in conservation should be replaced with "care" – and if you care for nature, you are coexisting. In Africa, the first steps towards coexistence should be for the human tribes, the black, the brown and white to finally accept their many differences, to learn to live with each other and to really know each other. In turn, we will then reap the knowledge of how to live again with other species.

Let us now look at a possible practical example of the lack of care. Recently, I undertook a survey of elephant movement areas outside two joint conservation areas in Botswana and Zimbabwe, which I collectively refer to as the Tuli bushlands. In July 1998, conservationists on the Botswana side of the bushlands instigated the capture of thirty elephant calves (forcibly removed from their family) for export and sale to an animal broker in South Africa (then to be destined for zoos and "wildlife parks" internationally). When the scandal broke, the conservationists attempted to use terms such as "elephant overpopulation" and "drought" as a justification for the forced removal. (Technically, because of the elephants' ability to freely cross into the Zimbabwe side of the bushlands and vice versa, they are regarded by international agreement as a joint resource of the two countries – yet the Zimbabwean government had not been consulted by the Botswana Government about the capture of elephant calves.)

The Tuli conservationists' decision to capture the elephants was, in my opinion, narrow sighted and not based on looking at the 'whole' picture. Such human narrow sightedness is, I believe, what Henry Beston was conveying when he wrote:

> Remote from universal nature and living in complicated artifice, man in civilization surveys the creature through the glass of his knowledge and sees thereby a feather magnified and the whole image in distortion.

Returning to the coexistence viewpoint, my elephant movement survey was intended to find out how and to where the elephants were moving, and to learn of their true range by looking at the big picture – and not surveying them through the glass, i.e. pinpointing only what is going on in one portion of their range – within the man defined boundary of the Tuli bushlands.

I had lived in the Tuli bushlands in the early 1980s as a game ranger. At that time I was studying the Tuli lions and I witnessed first hand what damage armed ivory poachers were inflicting upon the Tuli elephants. The deaths and lingering injuries were terrible. However, after the 1989 CITES ivory ban, the situation stabilized in the Tuli with regards to ivory poaching.

I know this because from 1989 to 1993, I embarked upon the re-introduction of the last lion orphans of George Adamson into the bushlands. Back in the Tuli again, after an absence of two and a half years, I soon noticed that ivory poaching had diminished dramatically and the elephant herds had become calmer.

I also learnt that the Tuli elephants were now beginning to move out of the confines of the bushlands' boundaries, moving again (and increasingly further afield as my survey was to show me) on what were surely ancestral range areas and migration routes.

However, despite knowing that the elephants had begun moving again in recent years, the findings of my survey came as a surprise. I learnt that south west of the Tuli, certain elephants had ranged over 100 km from the reserve. The easterly elephant movements were even further, and the north east, north and north western movements were so distant that I eventually could not be certain whether the elephant movements reported to me were that of Tuli elephants or elephants from the Hwange/Chobe National Parks system. In fact, I concluded that there must be an overlap of movement in both populations.

With the increased ranging of the Tuli elephants in recent years, there also seemed to be an increased conflict with man and his crops in certain areas. Though being sympathetic to the farmer's loss of crops to elephants, I am reminded of what Kenya's ex-wildlife Services Director David Western once wrote concerning traditional animal and human conflict in Africa:

> The farmers were stoical about the hardship they suffered from wild animals, but then protecting crops from animals was as much a part of their calendar as hoeing, weeding and harvesting.

In the Tuli elephant movement corridors, I discovered that drums and gunshots are often used to chase elephants from fields. Neither are totally effective deterrents. Crops are damaged and elephants are wounded or killed outright. Ideally, electrified fencing would provide a more effective solution.

This enables us to look at the situation with fresh eyes, and see the potential of the concept of coexistence. When I completed the Tuli elephant survey, I looked broadly at my findings.

The Tuli elephants were moving again, though tentatively on portions of their ancestral range. People existed too in these areas – but then, they always had. It was ancestral land for them too.

Studying my findings, I suddenly saw the potential of the formation of elephant movement "corridors", interlinking the Tuli bushlands in a transfrontier way with the Hwange, Gona-re-Zhou and Kruger systems. The elephants could be the catalysts to bridge the gaps separating the wildlife regions. Unlike the concept of game reserves, I saw no disposing of people to put aside land for wildlife. I saw a new/old concept, which we can call "coexistence". These potential "corridors of peace" – "Kagiso" Corridors (the Setswana word for "peace") would be man and wildlife corridors, linking four international wildlife areas; Hwange, Tuli, Kruger and Gona-re-Zhou.

Should the human inhabitants of this area see potential benefits in the proposed Kagiso Corridors, the prospect for man and wildlife would be enormous. "Ubuntu", is a word used in South Africa describing the African philosophy of "I am because I belong" – the basic essence of religious experience throughout Africa. "I am because I am part of, a part of every thing", could be Ubuntu's broadest definition. With the people's agreement on the establishment of the Kagiso areas, man and wildlife would be members again of a mutual constituency – Nature. "Maybe, in theory", I can hear the cynics say, and "But what about the practicalities of this Utopian vision?" Well, let's look at some broad practicalities and possibilities.

First, with the appointment of a small Kagiso team, well versed in wildlife issues and African cultural beliefs, the following should be undertaken:

1. Careful, tireless consultation should take place with all human constituents, chiefs, headmen, women's groups, rural councils, local MP's etc, of the proposed Kagiso areas. With grass root agreement of the Kagiso project achieved, this agreement must be taken to governmental level and in turn, joint governmental level (Zimbabwe, Botswana and South Africa), i.e. through the southern African development co-ordination conference (SADCC) which developed through the 1990s, a regional Natural Resource Policy and development strategy. This mechanism facilitates regional co-operation amongst SADCC member states in issues relating to natural resource development.
2. Research (for example, via satellite tracking) would then have to be undertaken to define (i) the international elephant corridors and where they might broaden in the future and (ii) the main areas of people/elephant conflict, i.e. areas of crop damage etc.
3. With (2) achieved, conflict areas would then have to be prioritized for electric fencing with instruction and back up for long term maintenance of equipment.
4. Areas for alternative water points should be identified and established in the Kagiso areas to further reduce man/elephant conflict, water provided where elephants can drink in winter months, i.e.

without them having to move into settlement areas as they presently do.
5. An aggressive joint marketing strategy and business plan would have to be established by all stakeholders to promote low impact tourism (non-consumptive) in the Kagiso areas, where networks of eco-camps could be set up and locally managed. The founding of a Kagiso Foundation, with an agreed upon constitution would formalize the project.

Afri-tourism, a cultural/wildlife based form of tourism would be at the heart of the Kagiso vision. The unique Afri-tourism features and selling points of the Kagiso areas would be:

- African elephants moving again in historical rangeland and on former-past migration routes.
- Incredible archaeological sites, from early stone-age sites to Mapungubwe – one of the most remarkable Iron Age sites in Southern Africa. Other archaeological sites in the Kagiso areas would include those of the Motloutse ruins, Domboshaba ruins and Thulamela – the 16th century excavated and reconstructed site in the Kruger National Park. Accessibility would also be possible to the majestic Matobo National Park, an important tourism area of Zimbabwe, which is rich in archaeological and cultural sites, as well as being a wildlife area. The Kagiso areas also have important and spectacular Bushmen paintings and there are significant dinosaur fossil sites along the Limpopo river.
- Colonial History, i.e. the forming of Fort Tuli and establishment of Rhodesia by Cecil John Rhodes and his Charter company – and how the descendants of the Matabele and Shona regained their land from the descendants of the colonists to form the nation of Zimbabwe.
- Sandstone geology, and caves
- Local culture and history with insights into:
  Traditional life (tourists could, for example stay at Kagiso initiated and community run, guest accommodation).
  Traditional African healing.
  Original environmental beliefs.
  Traditional African religions and cultural beliefs as well as other indigenous knowledge.
  Craft making and basket usage, traditional sculpture, carving arts etc.
- The accessibility of the Kagiso areas into internationally known wildlife areas (linked by the Kagiso areas), such as the Hwange National Park (Zimbabwe), the Tuli bushlands (Botswana/ Zimbabwe), Gona-re-Zhou (Zimbabwe), the Motobo National Park (Zimbabwe), the Kruger National Park (South Africa) and

the Limpopo Valley National Park (South Africa, and part of the proposed International Peace Park).

- Seasonal and annual utilization of three spectacular African rivers – the Limpopo, Shashe and the Motloutse. This could be combined with on-going wilderness trails, with canoe safaris from river fronting Kagiso Corridors eco-camps.
- The story of the Adamson lions. The rehabilitation of the last three lion orphans of 'Born Free' legend George Adamson, took place in the Tuli bushlands and where today, the descendants of these famous lions live on.
- The great diversity of birdlife, with bird species exceeding 400 in the potential Kagiso areas.

The Kagiso Transfrontier areas would additionally create:

- The unique opportunity to establish a transfrontier model of non-consumptive utilization and protection of wildlife – a partnership between indigenous communities, government agencies, NGOS, rural development agencies and district councils etc. to provide community and private sector "eco-friendly" opportunities. The learning process to forming such a model would lay foundations for future projects in Africa.
- The opportunity of establishing youth orientated Kagiso wildlife clubs, combining traditional and modern environmental beliefs in its working philosophy.
- The opportunity of establishing a system of Kagiso auxiliary game scouts from within the communities to undertake wildlife monitoring.
- The challenge of achieving greater harmony between wildlife and humans within the Kagiso areas.
- The potential to inject monies into the local economies of the Kagiso areas and integrating rural development, tourism and African coexistence.

A "Utopian dream . . . pie in the sky"? I do not believe so. I feel that the implementations of such initiatives are in fact essential for the future of Africa's wildlife and wild places. For example, it has been stated that on the basis of biological insights, it is known today that our present protected areas are themselves far too small and fragmented to prevent mass extinction. In contrast, the Kagiso transfrontier concept has the potential of creating the bridges across the chasms separating Africa's National Parks and reserves boundaries.

We need to again strive towards ensuring that it is natural and normal for wildlife to exist outside the parks and reserves. To do this it is essential to view man and wildlife as members of the mutual constituency namely – Nature. The future of Africa's wildlife is, I believe, dependent upon man's re-discovery of the African art of coexistence. In turn, co-existence needs to replace separatist conservation – and the world could learn from this art of co-existence. The world could learn from Africa.

The African people themselves, in particular the rural communities, would be the focus of the coexistence and the approach would be locally driven rather than national. In this vision, original cultural values would re-blossom and where needed, re-adapt to modern problems.

In times past in Africa, every tree, every spring, every stream and every hill had its own genius loci, its guardian spirit. However, with western domination of Africa and the lack of respect for African animistic beliefs by the colonialising westerners, it was made possible for nature to be exploited in a mood of indifference to the feeling of things natural. This needs to be reversed by the Africans.

Today, the damage is still being meted out, but will lessen if an Africanism encompassing a philosophy of respect and reverence for nature re-emerges. The beginning of this portion of the overall African renaissance is where we stand today. It will take time to grow, but at least today, we can have a vision for tomorrow, a tomorrow when co-existence can begin to take hold in our hearts and in turn replace conservation for the benefit of one whole – man in Nature.

The Contributors

Bill Jordan built up his own veterinary practice, which encompassed working at Chester Zoo. In 1964 he sold the practice to become consultant clinician to the Government of Iran. He later worked in South Africa before returning to the U.K. to found the wildlife department of the RSPCA. He founded the charity Care For the Wild in 1984. He has been consultant to the European Union on several wildlife directives, the British Government on whaling and animal trap standards, and British Airways. He wrote the guidelines for the transport of wild animals for the Convention on International Trade in Endangered Species (CITES) and is at present a consultant to the International Union for the Conservation of Nature (IUCN). He is a trustee of the Donkey Sanctuary and Compassion in World Farming and he was recently elected vice-president of the RSPCA. He is the author of 13 books and numerous articles on wildlife.

Lindsey Gillson is currently working on her D.Phil. at the University of Oxford. Her research is on the resilience of elephant habitat in Tsavo National Park, Kenya. Prior to this, she worked as a researcher for Care for the Wild International, working with Dr Bill Jordan on issues such as the ivory trade, tiger conservation and the fur trade. She also contributed to several Care for the Wild publications, including books on Tigers, Elephants and Badgers. She has an M.Sc. in Environmental Technology, from Imperial College, London, and a BA in Pure and Applied Biology from the University of Oxford.

Samantha Scott qualified from Bristol Veterinary School in 1988. Animal behaviour and welfare, and pain management including acupuncture, have been her fields of special interest for eight years. Samantha has reported on the welfare and behaviour of captive wild animals in UK, Eire and Canada for a number of welfare organizations. She lectures to undergraduates at Edinburgh and Glasgow Veterinary Schools on behaviour and ethology, and is the Honorary Veterinary Advisor to the Captive Animal Protection Society (CAPS).

Rob Laidlaw began his animal protection work in 1979 investigating killing methods in slaughterhouses, and animal husbandry and housing conditions in "factory farms". Since 1984, he has been involved in wildlife issues, with an emphasis on the welfare of wildlife in captivity. His work has resulted in an upgrading of zoo conditions across Canada and the closure of a number of substandard facilities. Mr Laidlaw currently serves as Executive Director of

Zoocheck Canada, where he is responsible for wildlife programmes and public awareness initiative. He lives in Toronto.

Credo Mutwa, well-known wise man of Africa and sanusi (uppermost sangome) of all sangomas in southern Africa, is respected and known by people across the world. His first book, *Indaba my Children*, brought him international acclaim and a huge following. His vast knowledge and erudition, combined with humility and a quiet sense of humour, have also made him a popular public speaker. In *Isilwane – The Animal*, Credo Mutwa's ability as a unique storyteller is revealed as he combines poetry and humour, tenderness and violence, factual information and mystic beliefs in a rare and most delightful way. He writes about a vast array of animals, from domestic pets and farmyard animals to lions, snakes and crocodiles, introducing each with a praise song, followed by traditional tales which provide insight into the myriad African traditions and beliefs surrounding each animal. Highly entertaining and eminently readable, the tales reveal the reverence in which animals are held according to African ritual and tradition.

Gareth Patterson lives in Africa where he has devoted his life to the protection of the lion and its wilderness home. He is the author of seven books on his life with lions.Two of these books (*Last of the Free* and *With My Soul Amongst Lions*) told of how after the death of "Born Free" legend George Adamson, Gareth rescued and returned to the wilds Adamson's last lion orphans in Botswana. (A detailed website about Gareth's work, books, articles, projects, documentaries etc. can be found at www.garethpatterson.com)

Index